D0024857

BFI TV Classics

BFI TV Classics is a series of books celebrating key individual television programmes and series. Television scholars, critics and novelists provide critical readings underpinned with careful research, alongside a personal response to the programme and a case for its 'classic' status.

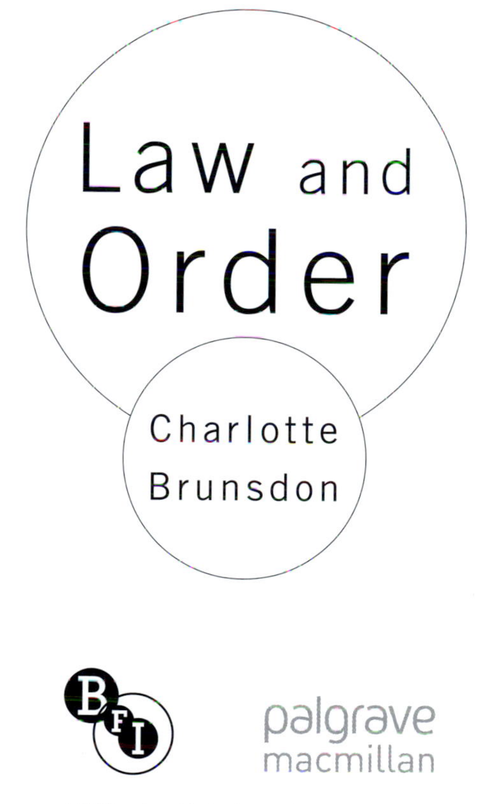

Law and Order

Charlotte Brunsdon

BFI

palgrave macmillan

A BFI book published by Palgrave Macmillan

First published in 2010 by
PALGRAVE MACMILLAN

on behalf of the

BRITISH FILM INSTITUTE
21 Stephen Street, London W1T 1LN
www.bfi.org.uk

There's more to discover about film and television through the BFI. Our world-renowned archive, cinemas, festivals, films, publications and learning resources are here to inspire you.

PALGRAVE MACMILLAN in the UK is an imprint of Macmillan Publishers Limited, registered in England, company number 785998, of Houndmills, Basingstoke, Hampshire RG21 6XS. Palgrave Macmillan in the US is a division of St Martin's Press LLC, 175 Fifth Avenue, New York, NY 10010. Palgrave Macmillan is the global academic imprint of the above companies and has companies and representatives throughout the world. Palgrave® and Macmillan® are registered trademarks in the United States, the United Kingdom, Europe and other countries.

Set by Cambrian Typesetters, Camberley, Surrey
Printed in China

This book is printed on paper suitable for recycling and made from fully managed and sustained forest sources. Logging, pulping and manufacturing processes are expected to conform to the environmental regulations of the country of origin.

British Library Cataloguing-in-Publication Data

A catalogue record for this book is available from the British Library

ISBN 978-1-84457-294-6

Contents

Acknowledgments

For such a short book, I have a long list of people to thank. I am grateful to Tony Garnett, Les Blair and G. F. Newman for seeing me and answering questions. They will not agree with all that I have written, but I hope they find that my account honours this project in which they were involved more than thirty years ago. Dick Hobbs, James Saunders and Lez Cooke were generous with their own expertise in these matters. I acknowledge the kind permission of the BBC Written Archives Centre in allowing me to quote from their files, and Louise North's assistance in this. Kathleen Dickson of the BFI's Research Viewings was enormously helpful, while Steve Tollervey was a staunch ally in my underworld screenings. Anne Birchall, Stella Bruzzi, Jon Burrows, Christine Geraghty, Jackie Hodgson, Tracey McVey, Rachel Moseley, Richard Perkins, Michael Piggott, Lynn Spigel and Helen Wheatley have all helped in different ways. It was a pleasure to work again with Rebecca Barden and Sophia Contento, and Rebecca organised some excellent readers for the manuscript, including Jason Jacobs and John Caughie, to whom I am particularly indebted. There will be those at home who will be very pleased to see the back of the 1970s, and, as ever, many thanks are due there too.

Introduction: The Original *Law and Order*

In April 1978, the BBC broadcast *Law and Order*, a series of four feature-length films about the British criminal justice system, which provoked uproar. The actor, Derek Martin, who played a corrupt Scotland Yard detective, recalls attending a football match at Stamford Bridge immediately after the broadcast of the first episode, and being frightened of going to the toilets at half-time because it was explained to him that the booing he had heard when he first appeared on the terraces was directed at him because of his role in the drama.[1] Over the four weeks of the broadcast, despite the immediate acclaim of reviewers such as Chris Dunkley in the *Financial Times* (8 April 1978), who observed that the series 'ought to cause exclamations of pleasure and praise over just about every aspect of the production', a wave of outraged complaint, in which representatives of the police and prison officers were particularly active, began to build. There was such a fuss – in newspapers, on television and in parliament – about the image of the police and prisons in the series that the BBC announced that it would neither repeat nor export the programmes. In May, the BBC was denounced in the House of Lords for having made 'a bad and grave mistake' in broadcasting the films.[2] The fuss rumbled on in the final months of the 1974–9 Labour government, and BBC personnel were not allowed into prisons for the rest of 1978, even to cover prison riots. Thirty years later, in April 2008, the National Film Theatre in London held a packed all-day event to mark the release of *Law and Order* on DVD, an event which was attended by many of the original cast and production staff, and which had the buzz of a celebratory reunion.

Until it was released on DVD in April 2008, *Law and Order* was one of the 'disappeared' of British television, existing mainly in memory and hearsay, and many people have no idea that the widely syndicated US series, *Law & Order* (1990–2010), in which each episode unrolls its crime story across two criminal justice institutions, the police and the lawcourts, had had a precedent on the BBC.[3] The BBC's *Law and Order*, written by G. F. Newman, directed by Les Blair and produced by Tony Garnett, focuses on the arrest, conviction and imprisonment of a fictional career criminal, Jack Lynn (Peter Dean), moving through the different institutions of the police, the criminal underworld, the legal and prison systems. Shot on celluloid, in a low-key, realist style, the titles of the films give an indication of how the narrative and point of view of the drama is structured: 'A Detective's Tale', 'A Villain's Tale', 'A Brief's Tale' and 'A Prisoner's Tale'. However, unlike the better-known US series – which now, confusingly, has a British franchise called *Law & Order UK* – the BBC films had neither good-looking police and legal teams fighting for justice, nor happy endings. Indeed, the 1970s London of *Law and Order* more closely anticipates the Baltimore of HBO's *The Wire* (2002–8) with its sense of the deep collusions of the institutions of criminal justice with the world of crime. *Law and Order*, like *The Wire*, takes its criminals seriously, and depicts its overlapping milieux in the vernacular.

It is not however, just widely syndicated US television series that are haunted by the BBC's 1978 *Law and Order.* Although mainly unseen, *Law and Order* has had a persistent ghostly presence in the histories of institutions (the BBC, the police), government (the Home Office, which was responsible for both the BBC and policing and the penal system), and, within television, in relation to one its most popular genres, the police/crime series, as well as the tradition of radical television drama. DVD release permits the scrutiny of old television in ways that were never anticipated by its makers and first broadcasters.

It is possible to linger over, to pause and replay, programmes that would normally have been watched only once in real time by audiences gathered in their living rooms. *Law and Order* can now be analysed as a polemical artwork which mobilises sound and vision to tell a series of overlapping stories about policing, villainy and the British penal system.

The initial broadcast of *Law and Order* is an exemplary case of television as a national event. Made by a public-service broadcaster, *Law and Order* provokes a reaction which dramatises questions about the nature of public-service broadcasting and its role in the *status quo*. The transmission provides an instance of the social and historical role of television as part of the public sphere in Britain in the late 1970s. Because of its topic, the criminal justice system and the resultant pressure on the BBC, it is also an instance through which to investigate the complex relationship between the government and the publicly funded broadcaster. Here, these relationships are partly manifest through arguments about dramatic form, and the extent to which what was seen as 'documentary style' necessarily tells the truth. Thus Shaun Sutton, the head of the Drama Group, found it necessary to observe, the day after transmission, that '*Law and Order* was a play not a documentary. Honest police officers had been portrayed in hundreds of episodes and plays on BBC television. In this case the portrayal of a dishonest one was a departure from the generality' (*Belfast Telegraph*, 7 April 1978). On the same day, the Chairman of the Police Federation joined the debate, observing: 'It's absolute fiction. They tried to make it look like a documentary. I would hope most people would treat it as the film that it is' (James Jardine, quoted in the *Daily Express*, 7 April 1978). The controversy about the programmes was partly conducted as a debate about form, in which popular understandings of terms such as play, documentary, film and fiction were negotiated by interested parties, often invoking an opposition between truthful 'documentary' in contrast to implicitly untruthful, fictional 'play' or 'film'.

However, interest in the form and style of *Law and Order* extends beyond polemics about the ethics of realist forms. For while on the one hand it is an example of innovative British television realism, on the other, it shows a sophisticated engagement with the conventions of television story-telling and the possibilities of this time-based medium. Its complicated, overlapping time scheme, and its narration of the same events from the viewpoints of different protagonists is continuous with the experimental thread of British television drama of the 1960s and 1970s. Work such as John Hopkins's quartet, *Talking to a Stranger* (BBC, 1966), an investigation of a suburban family Sunday, each play from the point of view of a different family member, had explored the formal and narrative possibilities of the television series as a dramatic form. These avant-garde aspects of *Law and Order* are complicated by its subject matter. Although *Law and Order* was transmitted in the BBC's 'Play for Today' slot, because of its theme, it referenced one of television's most popular genres, the police series. The resources and conventions of the single play (such as the use of film, calibre of script, adequate rehearsal time, intensity of a finite form) are deployed to render a world familiar from more markedly generic fiction such as the popular contemporary police series, *The Sweeney* (Thames, 1975–8). Familiar – but also here made strange: more difficult to follow, less predictable and more worrying. It was assumed that the audience for television plays was more tolerant of, and responsive to, textual difficulty and would be viewing for more than 'just' entertainment. What *Law and Order* does is to work over this generically familiar world of the television police series in which crime is detected, villains are caught, and the police can have a well-deserved joke or drink at the end of an episode. Although many men have drinks together in *Law and Order*, their camaraderie is never cosy in the way it is at the end of a serial drama episode, when, for example, Regan (John Thaw) and Carter (Dennis Waterman) (the protagonists of *The Sweeney*) retire to lick their wounds and fight for justice another day.

In the history of British television drama *Law and Order* is transitional between the single play and the series, but it is also positioned between 'high' or 'serious' television, and popular genre fiction, the television cop show. Its new availability makes it possible to reassess the ways in which we understand the history of British television drama and the genealogy of the popular crime series, to put it back into the histories from which its own turbulent arrival excised it. However, because the series exemplifies both the cultural and the social aspects of television, it is necessary to consider its aesthetics and politics within a series of different frames, from the broadcast schedule to the responsibilities of the Home Office. One of my arguments will be that *Law and Order* was scandalous not simply because of what it depicted in the individual films about the police, the courts and the prisons, but because of its use of the serial form to render a coherent journey through these institutions. Many individual narrative events in the films had readily available 'real-life' counterparts in the news media, from the conviction of the armed robber George Davis, which led to the 'George Davis Is Innocent' slogans still visible in parts of London, to police corruption trials and prison riots in Gartree (1972) and Hull (1976). *Law and Order* dares to join together all these different flashes of trouble in the criminal justice system; to imagine the trouble as systemic, rather than as a series of individual aberrations. In this, creative and polemical use is made of the series form to slowly accumulate the detail of the indictment.

Unlike many of the programmes discussed in this series of BFI books, *Law and Order* has been something of an absent television classic. It is a controversial, realist dramatic treatment of the British criminal justice system, which although unseen, had not been destroyed. It emerges from a specific institutional context, BBC television drama, at a particular time, the late 1970s, and speaks of, and to, these contexts, while seeking to intervene in broader cultural understandings of the criminal justice system as a set of interlocking institutions. In order to appreciate the intervention *Law and Order* makes, it is necessary to know a little about policing in Britain in the 1970s, and the way in which this policing was depicted on television, as well as the wider broadcasting environment, and these are the concerns of the first chapter. The second chapter considers the production context of the series, drawing on interviews with some of those involved. The longest part of the book, Chapter 3, presents a selective analysis of the four films which pays particular attention to questions of seeing and believing; how the separate episodes fit together; how the films give the impression of being 'real'; and how the audience's sympathies are solicited. Finally, using mainly BBC archive material, I examine the response to the broadcasts, what happened after April 1978, and particularly, the pressures on the BBC in relation to repeating and exporting the series.

The books in this series on television classics each make their cases in different ways for what a television classic might be. Some of the programmes discussed will be well known to readers, and gain classic status partly through a representative familiarity (*The Likely Lads*, BBC, 1964–6) while others, such as *Civilisation* (BBC, 1969), are recognised broadcasting landmarks ripe for revaluation. *Law and Order* is paradoxically recognised as a landmark in the television representation of the police, while lacking the everyday familiarity which makes Jack Regan (*The Sweeney*), Inspector Morse (John Thaw), or Gene Hunt (Philip Glenister in *Life on Mars*, 2006–7) icons of television policing. What I seek to do in this short book is to offer some of the contexts which will enable readers to understand why the series was such an event at the time, and why it has been unseen since. However, while providing contexts which allow us to understand *Law and Order* historically, I also want to argue that its presentation of policing within a broadly conceived criminal justice system gives it a place within a great tradition of television police drama to which a recent addition would be the widely lauded HBO series *The Wire*. For 'classic' is primarily a qualitative judgment, however that judgment is made, and I will be arguing that *Law and Order* rewards careful re-viewing because of its ambition, its accomplishment and its influence. *Law and Order* sets out to demonstrate how far the workings of the criminal justice system are from most people's ideas of justice and the law. This analysis of one set of interlocking institutions inaugurated events which can be seen to illuminate another set of institutional relationships, those between the BBC and the government. This is why *Law and Order* disappeared. The proof of the power of *Law and Order* has been the difficulty of seeing it, its persistence as ghost and rumour, as absent classic.

1 *Law and Order* in 1978: 'A tract for our squalid times'[4]

I remember the days when people would stop in, would not go out, because there was what they called a play, which was usually a film, on television that night.

Les Blair, *Criminal Minds*

So good I thought at first it was a documentary.

BBC Audience Research Report, 26 June 1978, p. 2

The 1970s in Britain have had a bad press in subsequent decades. The 1973 oil crisis, the miners' strikes, the three-day week, the Irish war, the failure of 'In Place of Strife', the rise of the National Front, apparently uncontrollable inflation, Britain's financial crisis with the IMF and the subsequent forced devaluation of the pound: all these are regularly invoked as symptoms of a nation in decline. This narrative of a decade in distress, with citizens writing by candlelight, television turned off at 10.30 pm, machine shops silenced, mass pickets and 'the pound in your pocket' worth a little less each month, has generated powerful images with which to justify the subsequent policies of many interested parties. And most resonant of all has been 'the winter of discontent', the name given to the cold winter of 1978–9, the last winter of the 1974–9 Labour government.

James Callaghan, Prime Minister since Harold Wilson's sudden resignation in 1976, had been expected to call an election in

October 1978. By some accounts, signs for Labour were quite good – the fact that this was difficult to believe is a token of the dominance of the 'winter of discontent' imagery – and North Sea oil was just about to be brought to the UK in serious quantities.[5] But Callaghan postponed the election, and over the next few months, a series of industrial disputes, many involving public-sector workers much affected by the combination of inflation and the government's income policy defined the decade, as Ford workers, truckers, nurses and binmen went on strike. Images of uncollected rubbish piled up on the streets and stories of blockades and queues, of patients unwashed and bodies unburied, filled the papers. The 'winter of discontent' gave Mrs Thatcher's Conservatives an opportunity they did not miss, just as, nearly twenty years later, it gave the New Labour project an agenda of abhorrence; the promoted novelty of the New Labour elected in 1997 was that it was nothing like the 1970s Labour Party. A 'declinist' narrative of the 1970s can serve different political agendas, and this tale of the 1970s, with its inevitable turn to Thatcherism, has dominated more complex stories in which different aspects of the decade have been explored. These include attention to the much greater social mobility and income equality of the 1970s, with the gap between richest and poorest in the country at its lowest since World War II or subsequently, and the rise of new social and political movements, particularly in relation to sexual politics and the new post-imperial identities forged in arenas from the Notting Hill Carnival to the Grunwick strike.[6]

Law and Order was broadcast in the spring of 1978, and is one of a number of radical dramas to come out of the BBC in the 1970s. Its transmission overlapped with a repeat of the controversial Loach/Garnett series about the 1926 General Strike, *Days of Hope* (originally broadcast 1975), and followed, earlier in the year, Jim Allen's angry play exploring social-service cuts in the context of the Queen's Silver Jubilee, *The Spongers* (BBC). Over on ITV in 1976, *Bill Brandt*, an eleven-part series written by the socialist dramatist Trevor Griffiths had followed the aspirations of a young, idealistic MP in Westminster. One of the challenges of watching these 1970s programmes in the twenty-first century lies in apprehending them as made before our understanding of the 1970s was structured through the imagery of the 'winter of discontent'. Thus, in the mid-1970s, the 'days of hope' could also refer to the possibility of a radical social transformation in the contemporary period; the 1970s were not simply a period of crisis and decline. In the case of *Law and Order*, the persistent, salacious misogyny of the depicted masculine cultures of police and villains has to be understood within a social context in which feminism was a vocal, headline-hitting movement. Racist jokes about Brixton by serving police officers demonstrate the taken-for-granted racism of police canteen culture, not collusion with it. Storylines about the manipulation of identification evidence, or the mistreatment of prisoners, mobilise, in fictional form, contemporary cases and incidents highlighted by campaigns that received wide publicity. Hindsight inflects a reading of *Law and Order* towards the symptomatic – of 1970s decline – as opposed to understanding it as a contemporary polemical intervention into media-led images of the police, and an indictment of the state institutions of law and order.

I do not want to suggest that we can somehow abolish the gap between then and now in viewing *Law and Order:* our position in history is as ineluctable as that of the films when first broadcast. But attention to the broadcasting context, the contemporary television representation of the police, and some of the news stories about the British criminal justice system in this period enable us to understand something of the ambition of *Law and Order* in 1978, and why it has subsequently remained so difficult to view. These four films set out to tell stories about policing, robbing, thief-taking, prosecution, trial and imprisonment in 1970s Britain, and do so in a laconic, observational style. The series explores the workings of the British criminal justice system through the story of one man, Jack Lynn, a career criminal whose specialism is 'blagging' – armed robbery. The structure of the series dedicates an episode to each of the overlapping institutional worlds of 'law and order', commencing with the police ('A Detective's Tale'), moving through the criminal underworld ('A Villain's Tale') to the courts ('A Brief's Tale') and finally prison ('A Prisoner's Tale'). Lynn does not appear in the first film, 'A Detective's Tale', although he is drawn to the attention of 'the detective', Fred Pyall, by one of his regular informants.[7] By the end of this first film, it has been determined that Lynn is a 'likely prospect' for a conviction. The second and third films, each grounded in the professional world of the 'villain' (Lynn) and the 'brief' (Alex Gladwell played by Ken Campbell), trace the manner in which Detective Inspector Pyall achieves this conviction, and the fourth, set in prison, shows Lynn appealing against his sentence, resistant to the authorities, but finally 'broken', resigned to serving out the remainder of his long prison term.

In terms of the familiar, comforting world of television crime – dominated in the mid-1970s by *The Sweeney* – the series makes two audacious moves. First, instead of posing police against criminals, it shows their worlds as deeply imbricated with each other, sharing a vocabulary, an economy (of 'earners' and 'it'll cost you'), and considerable cynicism about the system in which they are adversarially placed. The emphasis here is on deals, not car chases. Second, in the figure of Jack Lynn, G. F. Newman, the writer, creates a central character who is a successful armed robber and understands himself as 'a villain', but is, in the particular case for which Pyall orchestrates his conviction, not guilty. The set-up for the series, then, is a world in which no-one is simply innocent, and the viewer is gradually implicated in considering how dirty the business of crime prevention can be, what might be acceptable practices of policing, and the broader parameters within which crime and punishment are pursued. *Law and Order* does not engage in explicit debates about policing or the criminal justice system, instead offering a naturalist representation of a determining environment within which integrity is both punished and impossible to maintain. In 1978 this vision caused uproar, as it was intended to.

The Broadcasting Context

Law and Order was broadcast on Thursday evenings at 9.00 pm on BBC2 as part of the 'Play for Today' strand, with the *Radio Times*, the

BBC's weekly programme magazine, announcing a 'new series', 'Four films about the law: those who keep it, those who break it and those who live off it'.[8] This slot and billing is worth pausing over, as it summarises the institutional context of the production. *Law and Order* was produced by the BBC Drama Group, whose culturally prestigious products were usually referred to at this time as plays, even though, as in this case, shot completely on film and approximately the length of a standard feature film.[9] The broadcast opened with the 'Play for Today' titles, and, as has been seen, the head of the Drama Group, Shaun Sutton felt obliged to confirm that 'A Detective's Tale' was indeed a 'play'. However, the dramas were actually billed, by the BBC, in the 1978 *Radio Times* as 'films', and the phrasing of the description, 'those who keep it, those who break it and those who live off it', aspires to a tougher, harder, more working-class world than is connoted by 'play'. So the BBC, in its initial presentation of *Law and Order,* not only omits any references to plays, but also uses a term, 'film' which is both more accessible and is more easily associated with 'documentary'. These are choices which will return to haunt the BBC. In this book, I will follow this initial BBC billing, and refer to *Law and Order* as a 'series' of four films.

Law and Order was made by the BBC towards the end of the period when this institution structurally dominated British television. For people who have grown up with the multiple channels of satellite television and the ability to re-view and record at will, the living rooms of the 1970s, with their three national 'mixed programme' broadcast channels, BBC1, BBC2 (which had commenced broadcasting in 1964) and ITV (Independent Television which had national and regional opt-ins and outs), may seem rather quaint, but it was in this context that *Law and Order* was watched, and this context demands some elaboration in order to better understand the impact, and the aesthetics, of the programme. All television was broadcast terrestrially, and all was available to all viewers, with no further payment than the annual licence fee. As there was little programme choice, and considerable consensus between the broadcasters about the appropriate time for types of programmes such as news and sport, the desire to retain viewers was less frantically marked in the pace of programmes and the frequency of trailers. For example, programme credits were shown in full, on full screens, without continuity announcements or 'next time …' teasers running over them. Remote-control devices did not become commonplace until the 1980s, and so viewers could not just flick away. This in turn had aesthetic consequences, in that programmes were often slower, but could also display much more variable pace, able to assume that most viewers had been watching from the beginning and would stay till the end. The new availability of *Law and Order* in the twenty-first century enables us to see not just a story about 1970s policing, but also makes visible the aesthetic possibilities of national real-time broadcasting, most notably perhaps, the use of greater shot lengths and a slower pace.

Its place within the BBC evening reveals a fairly typical BBC2 mixed schedule for the late 1970s, in which drama is sandwiched between popular history and table tennis. Over on BBC1, the news was followed by a comedy programme. So in terms of BBC scheduling, the opening of the drama was the entertainment alternative to the news, while over on ITV, the documentary programme *This Week* ran at 9.30, followed by the news. The *Radio Times* highlighted an article by G. F. Newman, who is identified as an author of crime novels, in which he describes wanting 'to write a script which would show the police as they have never before been seen on the screen. To show them as I know them to be through personal experience …' and gives a clear exposition of his views about the interdependence of 'detectives and villains':

> They talk the same way, think the same way and often behave the same way. Without the solid contact there is between them, Old Bill couldn't function as well as he does. Without information, a detective might as well be a wolly directing traffic. Their prime source of information is the felonry. A villain with a grudge works it off by grassing another … . When they get caught bang to rights, they'll usually look to get a result anyway they can. Sometimes this means giving the filth an earner, often it means giving him a body.[10]

The *Radio Times* enters fully into Newman's insider persona, providing 'Forked Tongues: A Glossary of Underworld Slang Used in the Series' (taken from his novel, *Sir, You Bastard*), which defines a 'wolly' as 'uniformed policemen, especially constables', and 'the filth' as the CID (Criminal Investigation Department), thus ensuring that even the viewer of BBC plays who has never watched a police series understands the key status distinction between the elite world of the detective and the banal traffic-directing world of the uniformed policeman.

Domestic video-cassette recorders were not widely adopted until the 1980s, and so television was a much more ephemeral medium. This 'once-only' aspect of television had consequences in relation to the public debate about *Law and Order*. For there was a certain randomness about who had seen the programmes and was thus qualified to speak about them. This meant that there were many interested parties who discovered only after transmission that they were interested. One consequence was that the BBC had to arrange special viewings for those who subsequently attacked the broadcasts, such as the MP Eldon Griffiths, the spokesman for the Police Federation in parliament, and eventually one of the programmes' key antagonists.[11] A comparison with a case from the previous year is instructive, as the enormous public fuss about the failure to broadcast the 1977 Roy Minton/Alan Clarke play, *Scum*, was partly orchestrated through extra screenings. In this case, following the repeated postponement of transmission, unofficial, leaked screenings were organised by the producer Margaret Matheson for key opinion leaders (including, for example, the television critic Peter Fiddick, the broadcaster Melyvn Bragg and the playwright David Hare), although the play was not in fact broadcast until after Clarke's death in 1991.[12] This campaign, for which Matheson was reprimanded within the BBC, indicates the types of strategies necessary in pre-internet days, and had been pioneered by Tony Garnett in relation to 1960s 'Wednesday Plays' such as *Up the Junction* (BBC, 1965) and *Cathy Come Home* (BBC, 1966).[13] In this period, when any screening required the simultaneous co-presence of film and audience, the question of whether or not a programme would be repeated was more salient than it would be today, hence the enormous significance of this question to the BBC in the two years after *Law and Order*'s transmission.

The second aspect of the broadcasting context which is immediately relevant to *Law and Order*, and indeed, links *Law and Order* with *Scum*, is the relationship with the government. The programmes are produced by a Corporation which is funded by the British state through the licence fee, which is a variable sum set by the government of the day for a limited period. While the BBC is structurally independent of government – and much scholarship has been devoted to precisely what this means in practice – the government department which had responsibility for broadcasting was, in this period, the Home Office, which was also the department responsible for the police force and the penal system. So the same government department was ultimately responsible for both real and fictional police and prisons. The level of the licence fee – and thus the BBC's income – is set on a periodic basis, and throughout the history of the BBC, the period leading up to 'settlement' has been characterised by an understandable anxiety. In the late 1970s, this was particularly acute, because high inflation was most devastating for those, like the BBC, on fixed incomes.[14] *Law and Order* was broadcast in the final year of the Labour government which had postponed the renewal of the BBC Charter until after the report of the Annan Committee on the Future of Broadcasting, which would consider the allocation of the proposed fourth television channel and the level of service to be provided by existing broadcasters.[15] Annan reported in 1977, recommending that the proposed fourth channel be allocated to neither the BBC nor ITV. The licence fee announced in August 1977 was for twelve months only, and there was some uncertainty about how long the next settlement would be for. *Television Today* reports that the BBC was expecting the announcement to be between November 1978 and February 1979.[16] The government White Paper based on the Annan Report, which was published in July 1978, recommended that Home Office nominees should have places on new BBC 'Service Management Boards' which would have involved the government much more directly in the

Corporation. For the BBC there was thus more than the licence fee at stake when it was considering whether to repeat *Law and Order*. The Corporation in the second half of the 1970s was anxious about the terms on which the Charter would be renewed, the type of licence fee settlement which would eventually be made, and its independent place within the future broadcasting environment. The relevance of these matters for *Law and Order* is that there is unambiguous evidence that decisions about whether or not to repeat and export *Law and Order* were postponed until after the announcement of the licence fee settlement.

Law and Order is made towards the end of what is usually seen as the golden age of the single play in British television drama in the 1960s and 1970s, broadcast in the anthology formats of ABC's *Armchair Theatre* (1956–74) and the BBC's 'The Wednesday Play' (1964–70) and 'Play for Today' (1970–84). The history of British television drama has been told with particular emphasis on the way in which some of these productions, such as *Culloden* (1964), *Up the Junction* and *The Big Flame* (1969) used location shooting on 16mm film and techniques first pioneered in news and documentary work to create a new television realism. The political controversy engendered by these plays was often conducted as an argument about form, and whether it was appropriate for the BBC to sanction the use of techniques associated with the institutional commitment to 'objectivity' in often explicitly partisan drama. As this type of argument began to emerge in response to *Law and Order*, the BBC responds with the first ever edition of the arts programme *Arena* devoted to television, 'When Is a Play Not a Play?' This is transmitted on 17 April, between the second and third episodes of *Law and Order*, and is explicitly about the series, showing several extracts. The programme opens with the idea that people watch television distractedly, and that they might therefore mistake the genre and truth claims of what they watch, and introduces a guinea-pig family to watch *Law and Order*. This audience experiment is framed by case studies of what are variously called – in the programme – 'drama documentaries', 'dramatic reconstructions' and 'plays', which run from

Cathy Come Home to *The Naked Civil Servant* (Thames, 1975), by way of other contemporary *causes célèbres* such as *Scum*. Tony Garnett is staunch, thoughtful and unyielding in his defence of his programmes, as is Alan Clarke (the director of the untransmitted *Scum*), who offers the defining contrast that in documentaries people play themselves, while in dramas, actors are paid to play other people, thus rather elegantly avoiding the issue of the relative truth claims of the genres. Garnett will not yield the ground that *Law and Order* is untruthful, even though it is a drama, and refuses to line up factual and fictional programming respectively with truth and fiction. The family (in which only men speak) turns out to comprise sophisticated viewers, with one member suggesting that *Law and Order* does, from his own experience, seem truthful, while another suggests that the programme puts too many 'ifs' together. Alastair Milne, the BBC's Managing Director of Television, who discusses at some length the decision not to broadcast *Scum* in the previous year, mobilises what becomes a key defensive argument for the BBC: the question of how the work is publicised and identified, declaring that drama of this kind 'is only worrying if the labelling goes wrong … it turns entirely on the labelling'.

This *Arena* programme is an attempt by the BBC to 're-label' *Law and Order* as a play, to tie it securely into a genealogy of risk-taking, controversial at-the-time television drama. It is a confident programme, in which the diverse views of contributors of the calibre of Denis Mitchell, Jack Gold and Jim Allen indicate that although the BBC is conscious of, and anticipated, strong responses, these are familiar to a broadcaster with a track record in producing television drama which, if successful, should produce national debate. Arguably, and this programme wants to make this argument, this type of innovatory, contemporary drama is just what the licence fee should be spent on.

Law and Order and the television police series

It is one of the paradoxes of *Law and Order*'s history that its enormous impact on first transmission has kept it alive in discussions of policing, and media representations of the police, while it has faded from discussions of television drama. It even appears in textbooks about policing, such as Robert Reiner's *The Politics of the Police*, which describes G. F. Newman's work as 'the bleakest image of the police in popular fiction'.[17] The exclusion of *Law and Order* from the canon of 'serious television' is partly a consequence of its very considerable cultural resonance at the time of transmission –which has made it almost impossible to see – and partly because of its generic affiliations, which are that of the popular, less culturally prestigious police series.[18] However, it is impossible to understand the series' impact without understanding the complex way in which it both draws on, and sometimes repudiates, conventions of television drama both serious and popular, and in this section I will situate *Law and Order* in the history of the British television police series and ideas of policing and television genre. My argument, which is developed in Chapter 3, is that it is only because of characteristics that come from 'serious drama' traditions that *Law and Order* has been so iconic in the history of television police, but that this very influence, because it has been felt mainly in a popular genre, has been rendered invisible in the history of serious television drama. This in turn has meant that *Law and Order*'s combination of formal experimentation with television seriality has been forgotten.

Detectives, criminals and police have been a mainstay of broadcast fiction in many national broadcasting systems, and there has also been a lively international trade, with US series such as *Starsky and Hutch* (ABC; tx UK BBC1, 1976–81) and *Police Story* (Columbia; tx UK, ITV, 1974–80) popular in Britain in the 1970s, while British producers have specialised in the export of gentleman and lady detectives, from Sherlock Holmes to Agatha Christie. The history of the British police series, though, is interesting for the way in which certain characters have developed a resonance outside their fictional setting to become emblematic of styles of policing, and the history of the British television police series is often told through reference to three programmes. Thus the long-running BBC series *Dixon of Dock Green* (1955–76), which had a range of formats and transmission times, is seen to epitomise the 1950s, and the name of 'George Dixon' has come to signify a type of friendly and helpful neighbourhood policeman which many policy makers invoke as their ideal. This image of Dixon has persisted despite recognition, on his first appearance in the Ealing Studios film *The Blue Lamp* (1950) (by the film critic of *The Times*), that he represented 'an indulgent tradition' and acknowledgment by the former Commissioner of Police, Sir Robert Mark, that policing was 'a fairly rough and tough business' in the post-war period.[19]

If the inaugural figure in the British story is the bobby on the beat, George Dixon, in 1962 he is joined by rather more fallible colleagues in the motorised teams of *Z Cars* (BBC, 1962–78). The modernity of the 1960s is symbolised through the updating of the technologies of policing: patrol cars and radio links replace bicycles and beat patrols while the police themselves – controversially at the time – are shown with human failings. Set in a 'Newtown' northern setting, there is a self-conscious use of generic form as a way into a broader 'state of the nation' project. Thus John McGrath observed of the early *Z Cars*, 'The series was going to be a kind of documentary about people's lives in these areas, and the cops were incidental – they were the means of finding out about people's lives.'[20] The northern realism of *Z Cars*, which like *Dixon* is broadcast well into the 1970s, is in its turn disrupted by a return to the Metropolitan Police with the more action-orientated series about the Flying Squad, *The Sweeney. The Sweeney*, which is often seen, under the influence of vigilante films like *Dirty Harry* (1971), to have shifted the balance of ends and means in 'thief-taking', stars the plain-clothes, foul-mouthed cops Jack Regan and his sergeant Carter, regularly features car chases and guns, and is the obvious contemporary comparison for *Law and Order*.

Law and Order does not have the social range of a series like *Z Cars*; it has little concern with a wider presentation of 'people's lives', although it could be read allegorically as offering a cynical and disillusioned report on the state of the nation. However, its extremely detailed concern with the verisimilitude of police procedure – and the possibilities of 'working it' to achieve desired outcomes – makes an obvious claim to represent the real of policing. This reality of policing is significantly constructed against the world of *The Sweeney.* As Tony Garnett put it, 'We knew we didn't want to do a squealing tyres show',[21] and one of the key strategies of the first two films of *Law and Order* is the invocation of tropes and images that are familiar from the generic history of the British television police series, only to inflect them differently. Armed robbery was a significant peak within the crime landscape of 1960s and 1970s Britain,[22] and contemporary television police series such as *The Sweeney*, or the BBC's less successful competitor, *Target* (1977–8) return to the crime repeatedly; a 'hard' crime with a recognisable iconography of masked men, guns and getaway cars was an attractive option for television series seeking a male audience. *Law and Order* is structured through the planning (and aborting) of one armed robbery, and the conducting of another. However, in contrast to the customary anonymous and interchangeable robbers, *Law and Order* goes to great trouble to establish the milieu, character and personal life of its central 'villain', Jack Lynn. Similarly, in *Law and Order* notable attention is paid to the use and procuring of weapons. The police are shown as having to sign for hand guns which are issued for specific jobs, while for Jack Lynn, the weapons deal is a significant part of his business plan, and the price of guns is related, in 'A Villain's Tale', to the effect of the contemporary Irish 'Troubles' on the availability of weapons. This inclusion of the controversial topic of the IRA and terrorism – a sensitive subject for British television in this period – is an example of the 'serious-drama' origins of the films, the reference serving to lend a materialist backstory to the ubiquitous weapons of armed robbers in police series. It is through gestures such as these that *Law and Order* both claims its place in relation to the police series, but also disavows it, claiming instead to offer 'the real', rather than the generic.

But it is not just that events in a policeman's world are shown differently, or that the finite four-film series permits much greater freedom from the repeated structures demanded in long-running series, when the format itself begins to determine what is seen as plausible within the fictional world. There has also been a shift away from the vigilante morality of *The Sweeney* to a much more equivocal vision of a whole justice system in which the deal is dominant. For much as *The Sweeney* was criticised for its violence on first broadcast, the absolute integrity of Jack Regan was not in doubt. He was a rough, tough, enforcer of the law. Inspector Pyall was rather different – not so rough and not so honest. Long-running series demand engaging central characters who behave in predictable ways along with episode-length crime solutions. Pyall, as he is not returning every week in the way that Dixon, or Regan and Carter must, can be without redeeming features. His manner of working and his entrepreneurial initiative could not have formed the basis for a continuing series in the 1970s, but he was sufficiently recognisable to make it difficult to return to a pre-*Law and Order* representation of the CID without seeming simply implausible. After Pyall, it is not until another Tony Garnett production, *Between the Lines* (BBC, 1992–4), in the early 1990s, that the same dark themes emerge in the British police series, although one-off six-part series such as Troy Kennedy Martin's *Edge of Darkness* (BBC, 1985) and Ted Whitehead's 1985 *The Detective* (BBC) both offer accounts of the imbrication of the strong state and the security services. Instead, fictionally, the early 1980s are characterised by drama series which focus on new entrants to policing, in the form of women (*Juliet Bravo*, BBC, 1980–5, *The Gentle Touch*, LWT, 1980–4) and non-white males (*The Chinese Detective*, BBC, 1981–2, *Wolcott*, ATV, 1981), and a return to community policing with the soap-inflected *The Bill* (ITV, 1984–).

For the British television police series, *Law and Order* represents both a terminus, and a break, which confirms its 'absent-classic' status. The dramatic possibilities engendered by treating the police as part of the criminal justice system as a whole, the high production values and the standard of writing, acting and directing, radically alter the parameters for the representation of the police on TV. What is seen as realistic in the context of the police series is affected by a group of films which come out of the BBC Drama Group, and which do not have to conform to some of the institutional determinants of the longer-running series, particularly the working assumptions about the character and role of police officers and policing which govern returning heroes from Dixon to Regan. This effect is enhanced by subsequent events, particularly the election of the 1979 Conservative government, with its new agenda for policing, inaugurated by the granting of a full police pay rise on its accession to office.[23] Retrospectively, it is possible to argue that *Law and Order* marks the end of certain autonomies – for both the police and the BBC – because of the absolute centrality of a reimagining of the police to the Thatcherite project and its commitment to the market for the BBC.

Law and order in the 1970s: trouble with criminal justice[24]

In November 1969, on its front page, *The Times* broke a story about corruption in the Metropolitan Police headed, 'Tapes Reveal Planted Evidence: London Policemen in Bribe Allegations'.[25] The story was the first result of a period of surveillance by two reporters of meetings between a 'small-time professional criminal' and three detectives, documented with tapes, photographs and witness statements. This report, which memorably quoted DS Symonds of Camberwell CID saying, 'I'm in a little firm in a firm … anywhere in London I can get on the phone to someone I know I can trust, that talks the same as me …', began to outline the contours and practices of the 'firm within a firm' of corrupt officers within the Met.[26] Publication in a national newspaper, rather than submission of a lower-profile complaint to the police authorities, was a strategic decision based partly on the fact that it was the CID itself which was responsible for the investigation of complaints about police behaviour. The Metropolitan Police force numbered about 21,000 in total at this time, with 3,000 detectives, about 1,000 of whom were at Scotland Yard. The plain-clothes officers at the Yard were the elite of the force, working as specialists in designated squads dealing with Obscene Publications, Vice, Robbery and Drugs. Traditional CID methods involved considerable autonomy for individual detectives to pursue contacts and leads, often through inhabiting the same environment, and frequently drinking with, those who might be involved in crime. This policing culture, in which officers were to some extent embedded within the milieux which they were policing, and in which sources could be protected, was vulnerable to abuse – as is the case with all cultures of policing – and *The Times* case came to trial in 1972, which was also when Robert Mark was appointed as Commissioner of the Metropolitan Police.

Mark's confirmation as Commissioner followed a period in which he had been actively campaigning against what he saw as the corruption of the customary CID culture, while championing the uniformed branch. In origin a provincial officer, he was appointed with a clear remit to clean up the Met. To do this, he established a new specialist department, A10, to investigate all complaints against police officers, thus breaching the long tradition in which the detective branch, CID, investigated complaints against itself. Members of A10 were selected from both uniform and detective branches, and served for only two years in the unit. Mark's strategies, in addition to setting up A10, included rebalancing the relationship between the uniform branch and the CID by putting uniformed supervisors in charge over all divisional detectives and moving some detectives back into uniform; shifting responsibility for pornography from the Obscene Publications Squad to the uniform branch and rotating detectives more frequently. Following *The Times* case, there were two further major cases while Mark was in office, one against the Drug Squad, and one against the Obscene Publications Squad, both of which were proved to have offered some version of 'buy-back' schemes for favoured contacts. There were successful prosecutions against Met officers, some very senior, and a number of detectives took early retirement, sometimes on health grounds; in the period of Mark's tenure as Commissioner (he retires in 1977), 478 detectives left the force.

Law and Order was thus in development in the period during which Mark's impact on CID was at its height, and both Mark and A10 play a part in the drama. 'A Detective's Tale' identifies itself as set within the Robbery Squad at Scotland Yard, and there are hints that the culture of the detectives is under threat from 'the rubber-heel brigade'. There is concern within Inspector Pyall's Squad about one of their number, Maurice (David Sterne), who is advised to take early retirement, to 'save his pension' and a placard in the Squad Room declares 'Stop Arresting Innocent People': only on close examination is it possible to see 'A10' inserted at the top of the placard.

The most obvious reference to Mark occurs in the name of the prisoner whom Lynn (the protagonist of the 'villain's' and 'prisoner's tale') tries to help in 'A Prisoner's Tale'. Bobby Mark (Bruce White), a huge, strong man is desperately and violently resistant to the injection of a tranquilliser at the opening of the episode, and it is implied that he is not only upset, but mentally disturbed. It is only gradually that the viewer comes to appreciate that Bobby Mark's condition may be a result of his treatment, and that this fate awaits Jack Lynn if he continues to resist authority. Bobby Mark himself dies in prison after a final confrontation. The use of the familiar form, Bobby, which is not an abbreviation that a reading of Sir Robert Mark's autobiography suggests would be likely in his case, both disguises the allusion to the Commissioner, and is playfully disrespectful, while the fate of the character could be seen as vengeful.

A10 itself is embodied by DCI Chatt who appears in the first and final episodes. Chatt, played by Dominic Allan, is cast rather differently to the other actors in this first film. The distinctive feature of the casting of the detectives and the villains so far has been their interchangeability. Allan is more middle class in voice and demeanour, a pipe smoker, wearing brown suede shoes, and thus underlines the fact that A10 has a separate identity from CID. The A10 sequence is short, and consists of three scenes at the end of the first hour in which this possibility is explored and then exploded. The set-up is a scene in a police cell in which an active criminal, Brian Finch (Stanley Price), being held for questioning by Pyall, determines, in collaboration with his solicitor, Alex Gladwell (the brief of episode three), to 'do the filth right up', by appearing to consent to Pyall's demands for '£1,500 to drop you right out', but then to phone A10 to inform on the meeting. Finch's plight crystallises the situation of the career criminal within the practices of policing depicted, and anticipates Lynn's fate. He is caught between Pyall's dispassionate, turn-taking philosophy, 'We've got one in the book, we need a body, you've been elected' and his own lawyer's estimate of his situation, 'You're active, you've got a load of money you can't account for ...'. The desperate decision to involve A10 is followed immediately by a man in an office answering the phone with the words, 'Chief Inspector Chatt, A10'. This central scene, in which we clearly witness information about Pyall being passed to A10 is then followed by what we might call the let-down, when this same officer is filmed making an anonymous telephone call from a public phone box to warn Pyall. Chatt is filmed throughout with undemonstrative observational camera and minimal editing. The scene in his office is all one shot – of eighty-three seconds – filmed with two pans back and forth as he goes to the phone and then to get his jacket. This single shot, in which the camera follows the actor, poses the possibility that the outcome of the phone call is unpredictable. We witness Chatt reach for an internal phone book, we see him change his mind and prepare to leave the office, but it is not until he makes his own call from a public call box that the import of these movements becomes unambiguous. The scene plays with the viewer in relation to the integrity of A10.

Understanding the identity of A10 is important to the drama as a whole because Newman's implication is extremely provocative. Mark, appointed as a reforming outsider, who made pioneering use of the media, is on record throughout the 1970s as determined to break the power of the CID's 'firm within a firm' and to extinguish the corruption he saw as a direct consequence of traditional CID methods. In media appearances such as the BBC's *Dimbleby Memorial Lecture* in 1973 he discussed what he called 'the reality of criminal justice in London', impugning both detectives and lawyers.[27] That is, the Commissioner of the Metropolitan Police himself knows of the existence of detectives like Fred Pyall, and a series of cases in the 1970s exposed the corrupt

DCI Chatt (Dominic Allan) giving Pyall an anonymous tip off

proximity of police officers and the criminal milieu, particularly in relation to pornography in London, with revelations of regular screenings of confiscated blue films at Scotland Yard. So although 'A Detective's Tale' might be criticised for washing dirty linen in public, it was not as if no-one knew what was in the laundry basket. However, once the drama alleges that A10 too is corrupt, colluding with the very officers it is intended to investigate, then the success of Mark's project is called into doubt, and the resilience of long-established professional cultures seems confirmed. It is in this context that we must understand the prominent role of A10 in criticism of the BBC discussed in the final chapter.

Law and Order traverses some very volatile sites. It dramatises the criminal justice system in a period where continuing problems in the probity of the Metropolitan Police have been recognised both at the highest levels of government, and, more popularly, in campaigns to free those convicted on identification evidence such as George Davis (whose supporters gained enormous publicity via 'George Davis Is Innocent' graffiti at a range of high-profile sites) and George Ince (whose drug treatment in prison spurred a protest campaign).[28] There was increasing overcrowding in prisons (with riots in Gartree in 1972 and Hull in 1976), which threw into crisis the purpose of prison, despite the political importance of a 'law-and-order' agenda. The government had a very small majority, and appeared to have lost control of the country's economic future, which had particular consequences for the BBC on its government-granted fixed income. Television was the dominant, shared national cultural form, and programme-makers were not averse to criticising government institutions and policies.[29] At the same time, among the nation's most popular television programmes were the police action series, *The Sweeney*, and the prison-set situation comedy, *Porridge* (BBC, 1974–7). Millions of viewers tuned in each week to watch the Flying Squad catch the right villains, and the old lags in prison wittily and ingeniously make the best of their sentences. *Law and Order* set out to disrupt these comforting viewing rituals and must be understood across all these sites: the institutions of criminal justice, the institutions of broadcasting and the representation of crime, policing and punishment. Thus it enables us better to apprehend the role of television drama within national history and the aesthetic potential of television story-telling.

2 Production: Making It Real

You can't understand how this show got to be made without understanding that the BBC then was a very different animal to the BBC now.

Tony Garnett, *Criminal Minds*, 2008

Law and Order was made more than thirty years ago, and its enforced long absence from our screens, in combination with contemporary controversy, has lent it a legendary quality. All productions have their own mythologies, originally perhaps, informal anecdotes which participants have been called on to repeat in publicity interviews and career overviews. As Les Blair observed when I thanked him for seeing me: 'It's all been said before.'[30] This production generated two particular stories which different participants tell in different ways, but which always recur, and can be found on the DVD feature *Criminal Minds*. One is that there were 'real villains' working in the cast; the other is that police advisers were involved and paid, in some accounts, with banknotes in brown envelopes.[31] There is no reason to doubt the veracity of either of these tales, and that is not my purpose. What I am interested in is the way in which these stories work as they circulate around the programmes. For they confirm ideas about the reality of what was portrayed with their implication that the films partook of what they showed. These stories contribute to a presentation, and representation, of *Law and Order* as being so close to the world depicted that it was almost unmediated: a direct access to a shadowy underworld. This frisson of the real positions *Law and Order* within the distinctive London history of the traffic between the East End and the glitz of the West End, and what Les Blair, in a discussion of casting, called 'Joan Littlewood territory' to describe the overlapping of the worlds of crime and acting.

In this chapter, I want to explore the opposite. Not how unmediated our access to the world of the films is, but the labour of making it appear so, which would then make it plausible that some of the characters were played by 'real villains'. I am less concerned with whether there was funny business about Equity cards for non-professional actors (the actors' union, Equity, operated a closed shop, with no television work for non-union members), than with the creation of a world in which villains and policemen seem real – seem as if they could indeed be recruited from the worlds depicted. To do this, I will look at the context of the production and the work of its key makers: Tony Garnett, Les Blair and G. F. Newman.

Law and Order was Tony Garnett's last production for the BBC before he left for the USA in 1980. The series was two years in production, and by the time of its broadcast, and the ensuing fuss, Garnett already knew that he would not be renewing his contract at the BBC. He had produced *Law and Order* as one of a series of two-year production deals with the Corporation. In these deals, Garnett contracted to produce eight dramas over two years, four for BBC1 and four for BBC2. Within this overall commitment, Garnett (who was salaried) had considerable freedom about budget allocation. Garnett's room to manoeuvre, as regards both budgets and projects, was partly the result of the greater creative freedom afforded to producers within the Corporation at this period, but had also been won through his distinguished record since the 1960s. Garnett himself deployed what autonomy he possessed strategically in order to secure creative space for his collaborators. On this production, G. F. Newman recalls 'being left alone in Ireland' to write without interference.[32] Thus when Garnett explains, as cited in the epigraph above, that *Law and Order* was only possible because the BBC was then so different, it must be noted that Garnett himself, with international recognition for work such as *Up the Junction*, *Cathy Come Home* and *Kes* (1969), and a long history of more and less well-publicised battles with his superiors to produce engaged contemporary drama, was part of that difference.

The role of the producer is notoriously difficult to identify, and television scholarship has proved itself much more comfortable with assigning the authorship of dramas to writers – in this case G. F. Newman – or, on occasion, directors – here, Les Blair. Good television, though, is never made by less than a team and here I want to commence with the importance of Tony Garnett's role in bringing *Law and Order* to the screen. One of the difficulties of doing this is that good production is often invisible as it involves judgments, negotiations, organisation and management which enable the visible product, the work itself, to be made. Good production produces the work, itself fading from view. This point was very nicely made by Mike Leigh on the death in 2009 of his long-term producer in Thin Man Productions, Simon Channing Williams. Of the two, Leigh's name – as director – is the more widely known, but Leigh revealed that he and Channing Williams had a long-term gag about which of them was the organ grinder and which the monkey. On Channing Williams's death, Leigh generously observed that he could now definitively reveal that Channing Williams was 'the consummate organ grinder'.[33] Ken Loach, with whom, as is well known, Garnett worked as a producer, when asked whether Garnett's role was creative answered, 'Yes, particularly with the writers and the working over of a script, and in just being very shrewd about the project. Making the space in the BBC to get them done was also no mean feat.'[34] Les Blair, in the 1970s, acknowledged Garnett's creative contribution as follows, 'Tony Garnett's whole thing is to create the set-up which is going to let you get what you want from everyone, and he'll stick by that.'[35]

Vincent Porter, who has argued for the significance of the role of the producer within British film production, has suggested that 'although the guiding hand of a producer may be difficult to perceive in an individual film', it is discernible over time.[36] Internal BBC memos suggest that Garnett's work was clearly identifiable early in his career. In March 1966, Sydney Newman, the head of the Drama Group, used Garnett's name to identify a kind of drama, arguing for more money for 'thirteen Garnett-type productions', justified because 'the Garnetts were designed to provide the extra flash of orange every three weeks or so'.[37] Here we gain a sense that a 'Garnett' might not only have a certain look, requiring the more expensive use of location-shot film, but it would also provoke a certain reaction. The controversy over *Law and Order* is thus in some ways exactly what Garnett was contracted to produce.

John Caughie has suggested that '[i]n the best traditions of public service broadcasting … the canonical line of British television drama seems characteristically to place the real in the social', continuing '[c]haracters are not simply interesting as individual psychologies … but they function … as points of condensation for the social and the historical'.[38] Garnett's project, across four decades, is identifiably formed in this public-service commitment 'to place the real in the social', and *Law and Order* represents an interesting nodal point before his ten years in the USA. While there are many aspects of *Law and Order* which are characteristic of Garnett's earlier BBC work, such as the use of location filming and unknown actors to produce a sense of the real, it also formally anticipates the shift into long-form drama which becomes the dominant product of Island World and World Productions, the companies in which Garnett works on return from the USA in 1989. Thematically, though, *Law and Order* marks a move to a subject matter which is more explicitly generic. It is thus one of a number of works in which Garnett engages with the criminal justice system, adopting the generic conventions associated with the British television police series to explore the British state and the state of the nation. *Law and Order* is followed by *Between the Lines* which is set in a specialist police unit investigating police corruption, *The Cops* (1998–2001, World for BBC2) 'a show about the other side of Blair's paradise'[39], the prison-set *Buried* (2003 for Channel 4) starring Lennie James, and Steve Coombes's BBC3 series about criminal law, *Outlaws* (2004). Each of these is characterised by the placing of the real in the social, in that long-form drama is exploited to contextualise narratives of particular characters within a broader social and institutional analysis, often of a deeply pessimistic kind, if perhaps (until *Outlaws*), less cynical than *Law and Order*. The ambition of bringing serious work to large audiences also underlies the choices to work both in long-running series, and within the generic territory of fictions of crime and punishment.

In 1993 (during the success of *Between the Lines*) Garnett commented:

> I think the police shows ... – whenever they were popular – *Dixon of Dock Green, Z Cars*, right through *The Sweeney, Law and Order* and *Between the Lines* – ... the very choice of how their stories are told and what stories are told ... tell you a great deal about the attitude of the public towards the police at that particular time. And now, a mindless hostility to the police seems to me to be just as sterile as the 'occasional bad apple in the barrel and most of them are fine'. I think we've now reached a point where we can be much more sophisticated about our look at the police.[40]

He has been involved in the production of three significant television series about the British police which together can be seen to offer a developing meditation on the difficulties and contradictions involved in policing. *Law and Order*, which I am arguing, was a significant, transforming high – or low – point in the British televisual presentation of the police, makes the later series possible, but is itself more austere in its treatment of the police, less concerned with human foibles, and more with a systematic exposure of 'custom and practice' in the justice system. It is in some ways much narrower than later series like *The Cops*, although it does have the ambition to demonstrate the vertical penetration of corrupt practices, and their consequences, through the institutions of criminal justice, a set of concerns which recur in the work of the writer, G. F. Newman.

From his early work in the 1960s, through to his work in the twenty-first century, Garnett has shown a notable ability to identify and nurture talent in writers, directors and actors, and a commitment to finding new collaborators, providing initial opportunities for Mike Leigh and Les Blair in the early 1970s, through to producing *Beautiful Thing* (1996) for first-time director Hetty McDonald and *This Life* (BBC, 1996–7) for writer Amy Jenkins in the 1990s and *Attachments* (BBC, 2000–2) and *Buried* (Channel 4, 2003) in this century. His attentiveness to new work, his judgment and his nerve are significant elements in a production practice which has often challenged his collaborators to produce outstanding and innovative work. As Garnett describes it, and as his record confirms, 'If you give very talented people a challenge, they're usually able to rise to it.'[41] Stephen Lacey suggests that 'Garnett is one of a small group of television producers who have helped define what being a television producer is',[42] but Garnett himself is notably self-effacing in accounts of his work, rendering his labour transparent and describing his job as 'making sure I deliver everything to the camera'. The economy of this job description is matched by another understated description of a producer's task, in which he suggests that it is his role to ensure that 'you've got a crew who all understand the film they're making, and it's got to be the same film'. The simplicity of these definitions, the laconic insistence on the necessity of the 'same film', are indicative of a very experienced understanding of the difficulties involved in the undertaking to 'deliver everything to the camera', and point to hard-learned lessons worn lightly. In this context, it is worth noting the ambiguity of the job description given by Joe Shawcross, the socialist television producer in Trevor Griffiths's 1973 play *The Party* which has been widely understood to reference Garnett's milieu.[43] Joe, who works in 'the golden hutch at Would Not Lane' (the BBC Television Centre was in Wood Lane), exclaims, 'Me? I'm just a … producer. I don't actually *do* anything. I just set up the shows.'[44]

Setting up *Law and Order*, which was a large project requiring 'a big chunk of my budget', involved bringing together a writer new to television with a director who had not previously undertaken a project of this scale. The link between Garnett and G. F. Newman came through another significant creative figure in British television drama, Troy

Kennedy Martin (writer for *Z Cars* and *The Sweeney*). Newman had had great success with *Sir, You Bastard*, a 1970 novel about the rise of the unscrupulous Terry Snead from 'wolly' (uniformed policeman) through to the CID. Kennedy Martin and Newman worked together on a script for Garnett in the mid-1970s, 'this was to be the quintessential police film. It never got off the ground.'[45] As the titles of Newman's police novels suggest (the sequels included *You Flash Bastard*) Newman's police were some distance from *Dixon of Dock Green*, and the books were distinguished by the colloquial language and an insider feel. Some publicity at the time even suggested that Newman had been (a corrupt) serving officer.[46] In his account of the commissioning process, Garnett said he engages two criteria in relation to writers, 'Can they create a believable world?' and 'Do the characters come off the page?' Thus his initial criteria in relation to a writer are about the credibility and autonomy of the created world. As we shall see, it is precisely this combination of fiction and 'believable'-ness which is so central to the reception of *Law and Order*, as it has been for so much of the work with which Garnett has been associated. Garnett observes that when he looked at Newman's work, 'it sort of rang true'.

Newman had his own concerns in relation to realism, and was committed to forcing the public to confront the gap between television and actual police:

> I think most people have no conception of what policemen are like ... they just resist it, they don't want to know at all. It's a comfortable illusion they have that policemen are like Barlow or the man in *The Sweeney* and they do get the job done and they do make things safe for them.[47]

The view across the Terry Snead novels and *Law and Order* is that a 'susceptibility to corruption' was a necessary criterion for success in the CID. While Newman maintains that corruption in the Metropolitan Police in the 1970s was widespread, systematic and unavoidable, he considers his larger themes to be the similarity of police and criminals and the arbitrary and corrupting nature of institutional power.[48] In *Law and Order*, both these themes are explored across the institutions of criminal justice. Following *Law and Order*, other aspects of the welfare state attract his attention, child-care and fostering in a poignant play for BBC Pebble Mill, *Billy* (1979), and the NHS in another four-part series directed by Les Blair, *The Nation's Health* (Thames/Channel 4, 1982). However, it is police, prisons and criminal justice which recur in his work, both across institutions, as in the three-part *For the Greater Good* (BBC, 1991, prod. Kenith Trodd, d. Danny Boyle) (an apocalyptic vision of government in relation to AIDS in the prison system) and in single works, such as *Nineteen96* (BBC, 1989, d. Karl Francis), which has evident connections to the Stalker Inquiry into 'Shoot to Kill' policies in Northern Ireland, and *Black and Blue* (BBC, 1992), which deals with the imbrication of police corruption and racism. Newman is currently perhaps best known for the successful BBC1 series *Judge John Deed* (2001–) which stars Martin Shaw as the liberal, vegetarian judge, although he has also continued to write novels – such as the 2009 *Crime and Punishment* – and to develop a range of projects through his production company 'One-Eyed Dog Productions'. Newman has substantial control of 'The Judge', with a 'created, written and produced' credit, and this move into production is an attempt to retain greater control over his work than is granted to television writers. His role as a producer displays a well-articulated understanding of the business of writing and marketing television fiction as is demonstrated by his website <www.gfnewman.com>.

The director was Les Blair who had devised and directed his first film, *Blooming Youth*, in 1973.[49] Garnett had produced this portrait of the banal everyday life of a group of inarticulate, intense polytechnic students, which is quite wonderful in its evocation of the silences and misunderstandings of youth. The direction is at points so unobtrusive that it almost feels as if one is visiting their horrible shared flat. Blair's work in the mid-1970s, much of it made for BBC Pebble Mill in Birmingham, was already notable for the performances he could encourage from actors, as well as an attention to the detail of everyday life. For example, there is a moment in *The Enemy Within* (BBC, 1974) when a character, lovemaking interrupted and unexpectedly left alone, shows her desolation by having only enough energy to switch on a heater with her foot, demonstrating both the chill and the lassitude of the abandonment. Blair's subsequent work has taken in both television and film, and includes Jack Rosenthal's *London's Burning* (LWT, 1986), the feature from which the series was developed, as well as London-set films such as *Bad Behaviour* (1993) and *Bliss* (1995). His work is characterised by strong, intelligent ensemble performances within everyday milieux, and often a detailed and specific sense of place. Both of these characteristics are present in *Law and Order*, with the London of the films distinguished by locations such as pubs, snooker halls and late-night bars, overlapping and recurring across the episodes, as well as imaginative recourse to adventure playgrounds, netball courts and a bowling green. There is, however, less room for the other defining characteristic of Blair's work, which is its humour and compassion.

Garnett describes Blair's work as 'having a quality of not insisting', and judged it to be the perfect foil for Newman's shocking script. So the shaping decision for the series was Garnett's combination of Newman with Blair: shock and steadiness. 'Not insisting' is an interesting description in relation to film direction, a medium which is so often rendered very insistent through zooms, close-ups and editing, frequently with meanings anticipated and reinforced with music, allowing the viewer no space in which to reflect on what is shown. In *Criminal Minds*, Garnett discusses his choice as a strategic decision about how best to convince the audience of the truth of the script's unwelcome claims:

> I was faced with a dilemma. How do we produce this show in a way which will shock the audience, as indeed it ought to shock the audience, who don't really want to believe this because it's just much more comforting to believe these people are looking after us. I felt that the show ought to treat the corruption as a normality … it's so systematic that we don't even comment on it. I therefore needed it to be directed with the grain of that idea … Les has a very dry, matter of fact, laconic style.

Blair's 'dry, matter of fact, laconic style' allows characters to reveal themselves, and enables viewers to reach their own conclusions about these characters and their actions. 'Not insisting' becomes a stylistic strategy in which the director creates a world which could be interpreted in a certain way – in which certain meanings could be implied – but one in which these interpretations are neither enforced nor marked as shocking.

This has particular consequences in relation to the performance of Derek Martin as Inspector Pyall, who is, in his own way, also matter of fact and laconic. Newman's novels stress the importance of a CID officer learning not to let his facial expression reveal his feelings, and Martin's slightly fleshy face remains dispassionate through many interactions. At the same time, the character feels fully embodied; every steady shot of him walking down the corridors at the Yard, hand in pocket, or checking his surroundings when he arrives for meetings, shows a man who is a detective twenty-four hours a day. So the direction gives room for the performance – there is no sudden zooming into Martin's face to show his corrupt soul – but in each case both direction and performance seem to let the viewer make their own judgments about the type of man Pyall is, and what he is up to.

Blair's earliest work was in improvised theatre, and he had worked with actors to develop the characters in *Blooming Youth* and *The Enemy Within*. The line 'devised by' in the credits of several productions indicates his practice of improvisational methods to develop character, with certain actors, such as Philip Jackson, recurring across his oeuvre. His 1976 'Play for Today', *Bet Your Life* (BBC), which he devised and directed, is noteworthy in this context, as both Derek Martin and Peter Dean (who plays Jack Lynn) appear in small parts. So Blair was interested in, and committed to working seriously with actors, while Garnett already had a notable track record in casting non-professional actors. Their decision, for *Law and Order*, was to select mainly unknown and non-professional actors. In this way of working, casting cannot be accomplished on the basis of doing a quick test of some likely candidates from *Spotlight* (the trade directory of actors). Instead, the potential for a sustained and suitable performance has to be assessed almost from the beginning in the casting sessions. When I interviewed them, both Garnett and Blair separately emphasised how long they spent casting *Law and Order*, and how demanding this task was. Blair describes their casting strategy as aiming for 'that overlap between the worlds of acting and villainy', and in what Garnett describes as 'long, long, casting sessions', they would work on little improvisations with candidates, 'to see if they can be in the moment'. This work was informed by a sense of a continuity between the worlds of the police and villainy. G. F. Newman, in Blair's words, maintained that 'the police were the sensible villains, the sensible villains joined the police, the stupid ones did villainy'. Garnett recalls their thinking as, 'these villains, we'll either make them detectives or we'll make them villains', and it is evident, as for example, Derek Martin recounts in *Criminal Minds*, that the decision on which side of the law to employ certain candidates often came after the choice to employ them. Of all the performers, it was Ken Campbell who was best known, but mainly for theatrical and avant-garde performance work.[50] Peter Dean and Derek Martin, who have subsequently had great visibility in *EastEnders*, were virtually unknown in 1978.

The significant consequence of this casting strategy is that the CID characters are no more familiar to the audience than the villains. This runs against normal practice in the history of the television police series. Usually, while large numbers of unknown actors and extras pass through the programmes as criminals – and members of the public – the police, often better known to begin with, reappear each week, gaining authority through their familiarity. The police characters are reassuring because they are already known and always there. In *Law and Order*, the distinction between the two groups cannot be discerned through the relative familiarity of one group of actors. This in turn poses the radical proposition that the morality of characters should be judged by their behaviour, rather than by their status and profession. Newman's idea about the similarity of police and criminals is put into practice through casting little-known and non-professional actors who sometimes came from the demi-monde depicted.

The commitment to casting unfamiliar faces was matched by the decision to film outside the studio. The series was location shot with the exception of scenes in the Old Bailey, although with some difficulty, particularly in relation to the last episode, set in a prison. The Scotland Yard offices were replicated in an office block near Euston, and initially, the production team was refused permission to visit the Squad offices to see what they looked like. Through contacts of Newman's, however, the designer Austen Spriggs was taken over the offices on a Saturday. The level of the attention to detail in the production can be gauged by Les Blair's delight, more than thirty years later, in recounting that this research trip meant that the production staff not only knew how the desks were arranged and what the lighting was like, but they even knew the types of pen favoured by the Squad. For the third episode, the production took advantage of an existing Old Bailey set at Ealing Studios, but for the fourth, they were unable to gain access to a British prison. Garnett observed that 'the Home Office wouldn't be at all helpful about where to film'. This represented a significant problem, as the design of nineteenth-century British prisons is very distinctive, with the rows of cells tiered above each other on landings which open out onto a big central atrium from which all is visible. There is extensive use of specific materials, such as glazed brick and cast iron, as well as (more difficult to replicate) particular acoustics and sightlines. Finally, after a great deal of fruitless effort, the former reach of the British Empire, as Tony Garnett wryly noted, came to their aid, in the form of Kilmainin Gaol in Dublin, built according to the same panoptical principles – and also featured in *The Italian Job* (1969). This provided the location they needed, but at the cost of a considerable proportion of the overall budget. Again, though, there was evidence of obstruction when they were dressing this location. They had identified the firm that supplied prison furniture for British prisons, but were told very late in the day that their order could not be met because the firm had been informed that it would lose its government contract if it supplied the production.[51]

Les Blair remembers the eighteen months of *Law and Order* as the production, of his working life, which was 'most like what my father would call a real job'. This gives some indication of the scale of the project, while other factors such as the difficulties over where to shoot and the discretion engaged to shield the production from interference; the attention to detail exemplified in the prison furniture and Scotland Yard pens; the long hours spent trying to find unknown actors able to convince in their roles; each aspect of the long production, from script commission to pre-broadcast publicity, yield a sense of the labour involved in the production of the 'real' of television. *Law and Order* was made by a large team over a long period, and although it might look as if it just happened, it involved as much labour and artifice as the frocks and period setting of the literary adaptations which have proved a less troublesome, and more easily exportable, type of television. The sheepskin jackets and grubby macs of the characters are costumes too, even if they are the sort of costumes which make it plausible that the authenticity of the films was partly achieved through assistance from those really involved in the policing of the underworld.

3 Is This What You Mean by Law and Order?

Introduction

One way of describing what I was trying to do stylistically was to make something many perceived as shocking literally matter of fact.

Les Blair[52]

As we have seen, the recurrent anxiety expressed by critics of the series is that the films 'look real', and it is this, above all else, which drives them to fury. Protest about the way in which the police and prison officers are portrayed is expressed as anger about the mode of representation which is usually described as 'documentary-style'. The sense expressed is of being tricked – or of other, more vulnerable viewers, being tricked – into believing something which is untrue, as in this comment from the professional journal, *Stage and Television Today*: '[A] totally biased view of an institution … done with such a high degree of technical excellence, both in acting and production, as to make it very watchable and consequently very, very dangerous.'[53]

The programme-makers argued, then and subsequently, that it was not that their work was untrue, but that its truths were unwelcome. As I have already discussed in relation to policing in the 1970s and the creation of A10, it is now widely recognised that the Metropolitan Police in this period was deeply implicated in many of the practices depicted in these films, and Robert Mark himself was active in raising questions about the probity of some criminal lawyers. The distinguished criminal lawyer James Saunders has testified to the similarity between cases and incidents in the drama and 'real-life' cases in the period, notably those of George Davis and George Ince.[54] The overturning of judgments in a range of cases from the 1970s, such as, most notoriously, and outside London, the Birmingham Six, also testify to improper police handling of evidence, and clear instances in which judges privileged police evidence.

So my concern in this section is not with whether the propositions *Law and Order* makes about the social world are true; they have been proved to be true enough, and certainly more truthful than the response of the government (see next section). Here we might consider Garnett's definition of the work of dramatic fiction to offer 'distilled truth', or Margaret Matheson's scathing account of the *Panorama* reporter Tom Mangold's reaction to the borstal-set *Scum*:

> Milne [BBC Director of Television] showed the film to a couple of people … . And Tom Mangold said it wasn't true. His line was that it wasn't that any of these things couldn't happen in such an institution, it was that they couldn't all happen in the space of seventy-five minutes. Well, you think, 'Welcome to dramatic fiction!'[55]

The programme analyses below will concentrate particularly on the formal devices through which the dramatic fiction of *Law and Order* seeks to convince its viewers of the veracity of its stories. For the series does have a clear project. It takes, in its title, a phrase which had significant political currency in the period, and offers what seems initially a very expressionless investigation into what this might mean in practice in the streets, police stations, courts and prisons of Britain. To make this convincing, it uses aesthetic strategies which have developed, partly in response to current-affairs programmes such as *World in Action* (Granada, 1963–99), in devised drama and documentary drama. I am interested in teasing out, and analysing, the different ways in which the presentation of these four 'tales' whispers to the viewer, 'this is true …

this really happens … this is going on all the time'. In doing this, I am unpicking the achievements of the programmes. For the particular realist conventions that these programmes use, the way in which they are filmed and edited, were designed to be inconspicuous. As the director Leslie Blair observed, 'the easier it looks, the harder it was to do'.[56] This 'easy' look, as his comment indicates, is the product of its opposite, considerable ingenuity and effort. It is a directorial style which focuses on the unfolding drama of the characters, in which coherent, intelligent performance is privileged over flashy camerawork and editing. It is consequently a directorial style which is often underestimated as a product of direction: it looks as if it just happened. So a principal aim of the programme analysis is to demonstrate that *Law and Order* looked real because of a series of decisions made and difficulties overcome by its makers: it was not the result of leaving any concealed cameras running in pubs and prisons.

My proposition is that the 'event status' of *Law and Order* on first broadcast, which renders it a classic in one sense, has inhibited exploration of its aesthetic strategies and its innovatory combination of single film and television serial form. This, I will suggest, is most successful in the first two films in which the imbrication of the worlds of detective and villain is demonstrated formally through repeated scenes and a complex time scheme, while the third film, at moments, loses some of its hard-earned credibility by overstating its own case, and the fourth suffers a loss of dramatic tension. The line-up in the political argument in the 1970s about whether what was shown was true has meant that those who supported its critique of the justice system did not want, strategically, to engage with questions of aesthetic evaluation.[57] However, as history has proved it was 'true enough', we can now look at what does and doesn't work in the series, and how it achieves the effect that produced such strong responses. For this series engages the familiar forms of television, with their capacity to build an audience over weeks, to develop an understanding of the institutional structures of law and order. There is both a political and a formal ambition: to use the medium to show how different worlds connect.

The relations of the individual films to each other, and to the events depicted are at once cumulative, simultaneous and sequential. The time schemes of the first two films overlap significantly, while the second two are more simply sequential. The fate of the career criminal Jack Lynn and his movement from active 'villain' to 'broken' prisoner provide the overall narrative structure which can be outlined over the episodes as follows:

1. **DETECTIVE** The set-up: Jack Lynn in the frame as a 'likely prospect' for Inspector Pyall, with a raid planned in Putney.
2. **VILLAIN** The heist: pulled at Putney, farcical at Romford. Pyall makes his case, assisting identification of Lynn.
3. **BRIEF** The Old Bailey: securing a conviction of the innocent Lynn.
4. **PRISONER** The prison: from resistance to compliance: Lynn 'broken'.

Each episode has its own generic world: the police story, the heist movie, the courtroom drama and the prison film. These give a different feel to each episode – for example, the corridors and offices of the police procedural contrasted with the theatre of the courtroom – but, at the same time, the business of each world is shown, partly through stylistic continuities, to be both connected and very similar. Each protagonist moves through a series of meetings: seeking information, making deals and choosing strategies, in a series of locations, with a series of other individuals, some of whom overlap. There is a dawn police raid in the first film, and a robbery and car chase in the second, but in the main, the business of law and order, and indeed the business of villainy, are shown to be pretty much just that: a business, in which unmarked used notes circulate at all levels.

In what follows, the opening of each film is discussed in some detail, as it is here that a film must declare itself in a way which will entice viewers to watch. However, it is also in the beginnings that one of the formal constraints of the form – four interlocked films – exact recognition, in that, as the series proceeds, attention must be paid to both new and returning viewers. As contemporary and subsequent commentary suggests, this kind of representation of the British police and the underworld had never been seen before on British television. The power of this series comes partly from the authenticity of its language, the austerity of its colour palette, its camera positions, the length of the shots and the rigorous avoidance of music. This last is worth noting here in general terms, because as it is an absence, a decision made by Blair before production began, it is difficult to discuss in specific scenes. However we can speculate that the absence of musical emphasis, or counterpoint, leaves the viewer more on their own in terms of judging what they see. It also aligns the films with current affairs rather than melodrama. The absence of music makes its diegetic presence very powerful, and there is one moment in 'A Villain's Tale' when Jack Lynn turns on his car radio. He is parked in a multi-storey,

Jack Lynn (Peter Dean) listens to the radio after completing his arms deal

having just paid for, and received, the weapons for the job he is planning, and he sits in his car for a moment, quite still, listening to a burst of popular music. It is a moment of great simplicity: a man, in a car, listening to the radio. He seems so fully there as a character. And the music in its banality signifies something of his task done, his preparations completed, a moment of release.

I have sometimes selected a single shot for analysis, sometimes a character or scene. Through these choices, I trace the significance of evidence, visible and invisible, to the series as a whole. For these are stories composed of clues, traces, 'forensic', verbals (oral testimony), 'whispers', photographs, fingerprints and paper trails. They are about who knows what and who will be believed. Their most radical proposition is not that the police are corrupt – Ted Willis, the creator of *Dixon of Dock Green*, tried to get the BBC to allow him to raise this issue in the 1950s[58] – but that what counts for truth, and what is believed, is related to institutions, governments and power. Their reception enacted this very claim.

A Detective's Tale

Detective Inspector Fred Pyall spends much of the first episode of *Law and Order* waiting. The film opens with him waiting at St James's Park Underground station, and closes after he has waited outside a supermarket for an armed robbery that doesn't take place. Pyall, the episode suggests, is a patient man, whose expression rarely betrays his feelings. His characteristic posture, one hand in his pocket, even when walking, also suggests something kept in reserve, just as his caution about making promises or predictions, declaring that he will 'see how it shapes' indicates that he is involved in constant comparative monitoring of his enterprises.

And Pyall's patience, his confidence that things will 'shape', is the mode of watching in which the film tutors the viewer. For Pyall takes his time, attends to detail and performs his tasks methodically, but he is always busy – at one moment only just remembering to stop using his electric shaver before beginning to speak to his wife on the phone. He never rushes – but he also never rests. Similarly, the world set up in this first episode demands constant, careful attention. Almost every aspect of the practices and cultures of policing with which the series is concerned, as well as the foretelling of most narrative events, is laid out in these first eighty-five minutes. The episode is both complete in itself, a little slice of a Scotland Yard detective's life, with its initiatives, its trades, its successes and its frustrations, and a set-up for the series as a whole. And what is set up is the story of the fate of one villain, Jack Lynn, who does not actually appear, and a diagnosis of the workings of the criminal justice system. The viewer must share Pyall's patience, and maintain confidence that the details observed will 'shape' into a larger story. This attention to detail – potential clues – is one of the characteristic demands of the detective genre, and the good viewer is likely to be familiar with this way of viewing. However here, rather than permitting the viewer to identify the perpetrator of a crime, these accumulating details build up a portrait of a policing culture which is deeply, but apparently normally, corrupt.

It is the anatomy of this 'normal corruption' which is the purpose of the drama, and the tone and focus of this opening film is crucial. This is presented in 'A Detective's Tale' through a narrative structure akin to a 'day (fortnight) in the life' of Detective Inspector Pyall, which enables the viewer to become immersed in the everyday assumptions of the working culture of Scotland Yard. There are no big show-downs, there is no exciting climax – just a series of meetings, a raid and lots of office work. This depiction works off, and against, popular generic representation such as *The Sweeney*, by shifting the emphasis away from the action of 'thief-taking' to the much less spectacular practices of information-gathering and -trading. So Inspector Pyall is never shown running anywhere chasing anyone; instead, in locations ranging from police cells to pub toilets, he persuades criminals to give him names and details of jobs. The first fifteen minutes introduce Pyall's dealings with three potential informants, demonstrating his working methods, and their varied responses from established complicity to refusal to collaborate.

The opening scene is exemplary here, as it lays out the key concerns of the drama. It introduces characters and proposes future storylines, but it also introduces the style and pace of the story-telling, and invites the viewer to consider the kind of film they are watching. Like the best beginnings, this first scene condenses much that will follow and the texture of the scene, its detailed, but apparently casual, simplicity – two men meet on a train – summons the attention and curiosity which the viewer will need to understand the episode as a whole, and merits detailed discussion.

The opening credit of *Law and Order* is simply the title in white across the middle of a black screen. There is no music, and the next shot is of a London Underground train pulling out of a station. The camera is set up on one platform, focusing on a middle-aged man standing on the opposite one, so that the moving train intermittently reveals him standing in front of a station sign for St James's Park. This establishing shot, unambiguously identifies a London setting filmed in a real location. The use of location – given the considerable difficulty of filming on the London Underground – also immediately demonstrates the privileging of the authentic which will be a characteristic of the films. For viewers with knowledge of the power geography of London, the location of St James's Park station is precise: it is the station nearest New Scotland Yard and the Home Office.

The most notable feature of this first scene is its pace, and the way in which the experience of viewing seems to partake of the waiting and journey time depicted. Although not clarified until the dialogue starts, 'What, you miss one Micky?', the man on the platform is waiting not for a train, but for a man in a particular carriage of a train. The viewer doesn't quite realise this, but experiences it, waiting with him, as one train leaves, and the other arrives, the camera, first shooting through the train, then panning in the same position as he remains immobile. He waits, and you wait. You are waiting for something to start happening, for the story to begin. For you it is a beginning, but for

Detective Inspector Fred Pyall (Derek Martin) waiting

him, as becomes clear, it is an habitual and banal repetition. All of this is rendered quite slowly. Not in real time, but quite slowly, with it taking a full minute before the waiting man enters the train, so that there is, for the viewer, an experience of waiting, as well as its signification.

The naturalism of this opening scene – the observant, distanced camera, the location setting, the apparently natural lighting, the obscured view, the natural sound – serve to place the film within the traditions of 'serious' British television drama. It has a downbeat quality, a lack of self-declaration, which is not unlike the inconspicuousness of the waiting man, who may, or may not, turn out to be the central protagonist. However, its very realism – the pace of the edit, the way in which the train is filmed from an angle and height to show how it emerges from the tunnel, the slight camber of the track, the odd shine of the platform and the noise of its approach – is not the detail of the incidental, but of the highly wrought. This is that evocation of the real for which British television of the 1960s and 1970s is world famous, and which John Caughie has described as this television's 'aesthetics of immediacy'.[59]

After the man enters the train, the second title, 'A Detective's Tale', is shown. The combination of the two titles works to locate the scene within the traditions of the crime drama, and once that generic knowledge is activated, the representational terrain is rich. The detective, in suit and tie, with a side-parted conventional haircut, walks down the carriage watched in anticipation by a man in a full-length suede coat with long hair and a fashionable zipped open-neck top. Generic knowledge helps us recognise the scenario of an apparently chance meeting in a public place of a slightly ill-assorted pair, one in formal and one in casual clothing, the emerging business of crime, and identify the personae of an informant and the detective who runs him. All of this too is available in this beginning. But the conversation which the detective and Micky (Roy Sone) have on the tube, while it clearly sets up the key plot device of the planned raid on a supermarket by a known villain, takes place with the rhythms and noise of the tube journey constantly present. Just as our first sight of the detective was

Pyall's meeting with Micky Fielder (Ray Sone) on the Circle Line

intermittently interrupted by the passing tube train, so too is this conversation subject to the everyday life which surrounds it. The steady two-shot of Micky and the detective sitting at the end of the carriage is shot through the glass of one of the train's partitions and faint reflections pass over it as the doors open and close. This single set-up for the pair – held for nearly a minute in the first instance – is interspersed with other shots of their surroundings: laconic, quotidian images marked as Pyall's point of view as he monitors his surroundings while listening to Micky. The laughter of a group of passengers, a random Peter Gabriel poster in front of the open tube doors, the stopping and starting of the train, all claim attention. So the generic policeman/informant conversation is strongly contextualised within a particular journey on a particular Circle Line train. This is what I mean by 'detailed, apparently casual simplicity'. There is a clear generic trope evoked, but with a wealth of incidental detail which has no narrative significance other than to contribute to the plausibility of these two characters and the realism of their meeting. These 'extra' shots, such as the Peter Gabriel poster, set the scene in the context of the banal and everyday, embed the meeting within a broader panorama of London life, offering guarantees of authenticity by their very irrelevance.

And so the opening scene sets up two groups of questions. First, there are narrative enigmas, which are about the significance in what is to come of Jack Lynn, 'the blagger out of Kentish Town' and the planned supermarket raid, and also, perhaps, Micky's fate, considering the minatory farewell: 'mind how you go'. Second, there is a different kind of question, which is about genre and expectation: what type of drama is this? Is this a police drama? Is it a 'Wednesday Play'? What are the generic boundaries and the aesthetic inheritances which will allow us to understand what is likely or possible or credible in this contemporary 1978 world?

This generic uncertainty is maintained in the next few scenes as the story unfolds across some very familiar police-series territory, while at the same time rendering each scene with the same laconic camera and inclusion of incidental detail which impedes a simple narrative scan of the image to find out what happens next. So, in genre terms, the next scenes, after the opening with the informant, are the back at the station/paperwork scene, the drinks with the boys scene, followed by the action briefing scene, the dawn raid, the struggle/capture, the search of the criminal's property and the police-station interrogation. These are deeply familiar generic tropes, but the way they are handled unsettles their generic familiarity. For example, when we see Pyall in the Scotland Yard offices – which are not identified as the Yard until he goes for a drink – he is shown to take paperwork quite seriously. He understands about the value of records, and seeks information from files held as he pursues the lead about Jack Lynn. The Squad Office is dressed to be so full of furniture and men that it is almost possible to smell its atmosphere of not-quite-clean jackets and smoke and body odour and dust. Both Inspector Pyall and the camera must squeeze in – and neither stays long. Similarly, rather than being a lone seeker after justice against bureaucracy, Pyall's relationships with his superiors are co-operative. He is recognisably in the same game as them: to maximise successful prosecutions of known offenders, and this involves seeking and accepting advice.

In another example, in the search of the Harding house which follows the dawn raid, attention is paid to the dimensions and disposition of the house itself. It becomes more than just a setting for the discovery of a concealed gun. The smallness of the terraced house is emphasised by the way in which it is filmed. The detectives fill up the spaces: we never see a full-length shot of Clifford Harding (Alan Ford) or his wife, they are crammed into the frame, the disruption to their lives thus shown spatially, and through the constant off-screen noise of the children crying. Searching the kitchen jams one detective between a cupboard and the fridge, the shot only possible through the doorway with the cupboard door removed, as the grey early morning light creeps in through the kitchen window. The trendy wallpaper in the living room frames the defeated Clifford as he sits on the sofa inspecting the scratches on his arm incurred in his escape bid. The aspiration of the wallpaper is a poor compensation for the prospect of a prison sentence.

Scenes are not shot and edited in a way that allows for a simple narrative reading; there is too much there, too much detail, too much time. So, the good viewer of detective fiction is forced to ask about the purpose of this 'too much'. Its purpose, like the Peter Gabriel poster in the tube scene, is to guarantee the authenticity of what we see. These miscellaneous details, like the grubby painted hardboard blocking the chimney in the Hardings' house, or the poster for the Scotland Yard Disco Dance in the bar, or the beauty of the pre-dawn shot in the deserted London street just before the raid, create a world which pre-exists the story being told, and will continue afterwards. And the reality of this pre-existing world lends credibility to the story. So while in one sense, genre guides the viewer through some of the obscurities of the interconnections of the plot, on the other, the visual style of the piece repudiates these generic references, implying that this story is not like that, this is real.

One aspect of treating the corruption which is the theme of the piece 'as a normality' is this kind of direction, which Garnett, in assembling the team, consciously selected. The deployment of what seems to be a passive, impartial camera which does not swoop in for effect, and an editing style which rarely dramatises events, seems to allow the events themselves to take place. This is the patient establishment of a world in which the viewer must discern what is happening, and its significance. Thus much of the evidence of the taken-for-granted corrupt practices of the police emerges as collateral detail: questions asked (such as Micky's query as to whether Pyall can do anything with some stolen American Express cheques), knowledge passed on ('I hear he's bunging a DS out of Paddington'), little bits of work gossip ('I told him to resign, save his pension'), and gestures made without comment, such as the care taken not to leave incriminating phone messages as waste paper in the A10 sequence already discussed.

'Dirty, rotten grass': Micky Fielder, Clifford Harding and Terry Clark

The recasting of the familiar tales of law and order achieved in the series is partly organised through making the role of the criminal informant central, and demonstrating the necessity of the exchange and extortion of information to these practices of policing. The generic heroism of the detective, deducing culpability from clues, is replaced by the detective as information-broker. However, the films also demonstrate how labile this category of 'informant' is, how many within a criminal milieu become implicated in the trading of information, and the many different modalities of informing that exist. Instead of limiting 'grassing' to 'snouts' who conform to the rhetorical stereotype of the 'dirty, rotten, grass', the series instead captures both the precarious status of the informant and the fact that many in the criminal milieu resort to this role as a survival tactic.

One of the devices enlisted to demonstrate how this form of policing works is to show Pyall with a range of contacts: an established grass, Micky Fielder (who is a house-breaker, not an armed robber), a senior armed robber (who is paying Pyall off: more below), an older man claiming an insurance reward under Pyall's tutelage, and a prisoner awaiting a preliminary hearing in court. This spectrum of past, present and future information, which Pyall is shown to manage with brisk exhortations such as 'You help the system and the system helps you', also offers snapshots of different stages in criminal career paths, from the time on bail 'to do a bit of villainy to provide for your family', to the pathetic pension of the insurance claim. In addition to Fielder, I will discuss the treatment of two other characters, Terry Clark (Charles Cork) and Clifford Harding, to show the gradations of Pyall's information-harvesting, and the complex ecology of the world within which he moves.

The opening meeting with Micky Fielder is the first of four in the 'Detective's Tale', with the second one also taking place in the front carriage of a Circle Line Underground train. This regular meet, and a short scene in which Fielder is shown to phone Pyall's home, establish Fielder as a regular source for Pyall. In return for information, Fielder is paid, but is also offered some protection. Pyall's parting comment at the end of the first scene is an injunction to 'mind how you go', as he doesn't 'want to have to spring you from some local nick'. It is just this which Pyall must do before the end of the film, illuminating police officers' shared culture in which grasses such as Fielder function as tokens for exchange, valuable while plausibly active, but then willingly rendered up to bolster arrest rates.

The already developed relationship between Pyall and Fielder, which most obviously takes the form of a lubricious masculine camaraderie, but extends to Pyall visiting Fielder in hospital in the second episode, provides an example of an established police/informant association. One of the roots of Pyall's power, it becomes evident, is his astute judgment about how to play his sources, and his assessment of their reliability. He names Fielder as one of his best, and it is to Fielder that the residue of a political analysis is given. In comparison to some of Garnett's earlier productions, this series is deeply politically pessimistic, but a glimpse of a ghost of an analysis of capitalism itself as a criminal system is present when Fielder, sniffing around his Jack Lynn lead, comes up with the suggestion that a 'West End' figure, James Davies, who deals in shares, might be involved, observing that 'to earn money at share dealing you've got to be well and truly bent'. 'Isn't he always in the financial pages?' asks Pyall's boss, before shying away from cross-class trouble and recommending that the working-class man, Lynn, 'is more of a prospect'.

Clifford Harding is the second underworld figure introduced in the 'Detective's Tale', taken in for questioning after a gun is found during the dawn raid at the beginning of the film. The first words Harding speaks, 'All right, all right, I'll come', as he is being manhandled, caught after he jumped out of a back window, anticipate the reluctant co-operation into which he is coerced as the drama progresses. Captured wearing jeans and a vest, Harding is physically slighter than the policemen who fill his house, and his physical vulnerability, his bare white arms contrasting with their jackets, intimates his fate. Unlike the other grass, Micky Fielder, who is already informing when we first see him, with Harding, we watch Inspector Pyall 'turn' him. His career as an informant is shown from its inception, when his desperation not to return to prison makes him vulnerable to Pyall's pressure. In this first episode, Harding is the only character shown to have a home and family. While we witness Pyall lying to his wife, and his sergeant, intending to 'pick up some old tom [prostitute]' on a free evening, Harding is shown first at home, and then twice in an adventure playground looking after his children. It is, in the world of the drama, this humanity which makes him vulnerable. He functions throughout the first three episodes as 'small fry', used to reel in the bigger prey like Lynn. Harding's story, while serving the plot function of furnishing information about, and eventually testimony against, Jack Lynn, serves the wider theme by illustrating what might be entailed in 'being co-operative' or 'assisting the police in their inquiries'. If Fielder first puts Lynn in the frame, it then becomes Harding who has a personal motive to discover more about Lynn's plans, in order to retain his own liberty.

The third villain of the opening section is Terry Clark, who is declaratively unco-operative. Initially, the significance of this refusal to co-operate seems simply to contrast directly with Harding, picked up on the same raid, held in the same station, the two men played against each other by Pyall. However later in the film, when Pyall picks up a bribe from senior villain Maurice Dickenson (Steve Kelly) in a pub, it becomes clear that Terry Clark was 'sold' to Pyall. The irony of Clark's resistance, which has been shown in some detail becomes clear. It is because Clark can be depended on not to talk, to be 'as good as gold', that he can be fingered as part of the tax that Pyall demands; his honour is a reliable currency.

We are first introduced to Terry Clark after the dawn raid when he sits shivering in a police cell in his underpants. The constraints of shooting within the cell serve to make the scene feel as cramped as the cell. The longest shots possible can only be taken from the doorway, and so can only cover entrances and exits. It is not possible to get the whole of anyone in the image, so bodies are cropped, and the leather-jacketed shoulder of one policeman recurs in more than one shot. Clark's naked flesh contrasts with the shiny cell tiles and the fully clothed policemen, all wearing outdoor garments, while Pyall and Clark engage in a practised exchange about the contacting of Clark's solicitor, and Clark is ribbed about his 'choice of going away clothes'. The tone is one of tired familiarity, each participant playing practised moves: Clark is clearly known to Pyall, who presses him for information, and Clark knows that there will be resistance to phoning his solicitor, so names the brief as his alibi. This almost collegial familiarity is suddenly ruptured when Pyall swoops to grab Clark by the balls, his movement caught in a cut to a close-up of his hand and the orange Jockey Y-fronts. The shot just anticipates the movement, but the brutal gesture is so swift, with the detail of the modern, fashionably coloured pants and the grasping hand, quickly covered by Clark's own, defensive hands, that it seems as if the camera has captured the reality of Pyall's power. The normality of this

Pyall's point of view as he enters the cell where Terry Clark (Charles Cork) is being held

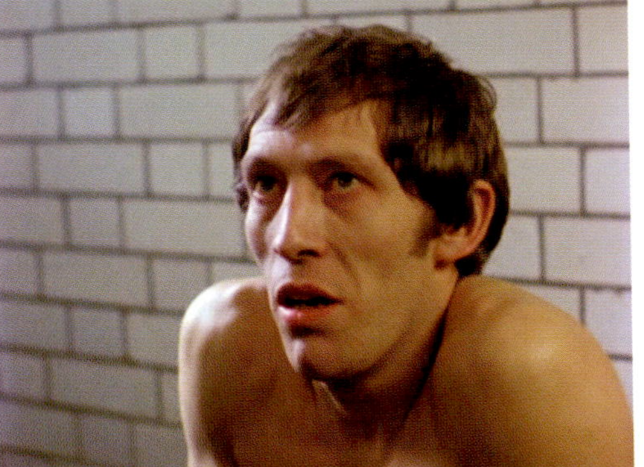

'I was with my brief, wasn't I, why don't you give him a bell?'

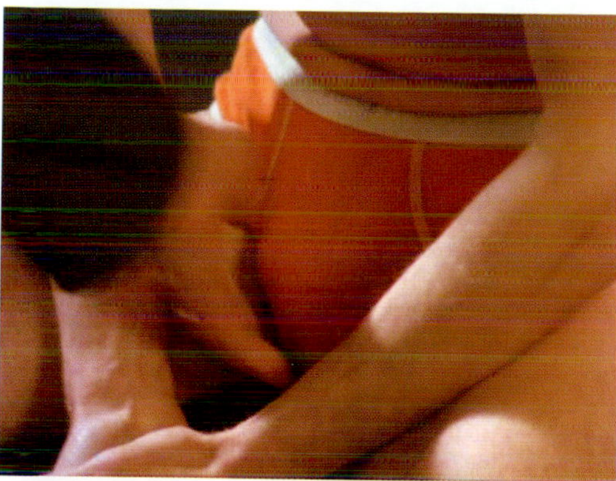

'Excuse me, Sir'

The sergeant's point of view from the cell door

behaviour is then emphasised by a cut to the cell door where the station sergeant appears with a message for Pyall. The sergeant, through a point-of-view shot which repeats Pyall's entry, is shown to see clearly that Pyall has pulled Clark to standing by his balls, but no expression crosses his face as he commences his message, 'Excuse me, sir', and we see Clark, in pain, sink back to sitting. The fact that this uniformed officer fails to react works to confirm complicity with Pyall's methods, their normality, and also disrupts the conventional reassuring familiarity of desk sergeants in police series.

This scene is significant formally, narratively, and for what it comes to represent. Stylistically, its combination of Newman's script with Blair's shooting style, which recognises the real constraints of the location, and the fresh performances of the unfamiliar actors brings together the key components in the authenticity of the film. The sudden close-up of Clark's body is shocking not just because of Pyall's grab, but because, in its emphasis, it is cinematically so unlike the film up to this point. Pyall, unlike Jack Regan of *The Sweeney*, does not deal in physical violence, and so it is ironic that it is this scene that is most often used when *Law and Order* is cited in subsequent histories of the television crime series (see the end of this chapter). The ritualistic quality of this scene, in which all participants show themselves to be familiar with their respective roles is not only significant for its revelation about the shared culture of police and villains. It also helps the audience to understand the model of policing which is being employed, in which Pyall is a recognised master. The explicit calculation of odds in relation to the trading of names, the recognition that all are involved in a highly structured mode of gaming, proposes the detective's tale as one in which moves are made at a formal, rather than a factual level. As Pyall's superior reminds his men before they go out on their dawn raid: 'Now remember, none of these men may have any connection with the Walthamstow … . They're all at it, of course.' This is, in one sense, a statement about 'the usual suspects', but it also shows the logic which underlies the model of policing here depicted. For if they are 'all at it', how much does it matter of what precisely they are convicted?

A Villain's Tale

But Cath, I'm a villain .... (Jack Lynn to his wife)

'A Villain's Tale' focuses on the Jack Lynn, the 'blagger out of Kentish Town' who had been identified as a possible target for police investigation in the first film. It falls into roughly three parts: the introduction of the villain, arguably the most sympathetic character in the series; the farcical Romford job in which both police and villains are made to look incompetent; and the final act, prosecuting the Romford raid. The introduction of Lynn is the longest part of the episode, taking up the first half hour, and here Lynn is in nearly every scene, shown working, socialising and with his wife and children. The second part of the film catches up, temporally, with the end of the first episode (discussed in more length below), and introduces a quite complicated story about a raid on a gas showroom being carried out by Jack's friend, John Tully (Barry Summerford). In the final part of the episode, Inspector Pyall returns to pre-eminence and is shown to orchestrate the action of a criminal prosecution rather as a film director might direct the action, organising props and scripts. Lynn's role shifts throughout the eighty minutes from being the initiating agent of the first part to being trapped by the end, and this shift is anticipated through frame composition, so that Lynn is shown caught within frames composed of car windscreens, snooker lamps and rearview mirrors. He is though, also, noticeably mobile in the first part of the film, and living a much more sensuous life than the members of CID in the preceding film.

This second film is, in plot terms, the core of the series. The central protagonist of the first film, Pyall, is matched with his quarry and antagonist, Lynn, who is shown in his prime, living the life armed robbery has bought him. The audience is shown that Lynn is not involved in the botched raid which then comes to court, and thus his innocence for the next two films, in court and prison, is established. It is also the film which reveals that the time scheme of the series is not going to be simply sequential, and is most radical in its use of re-filmed scenes. At the same time, this is the film which fully acknowledges the conventions of the police-action series, and offers masked men, guns, a raid and a location-filmed car chase. In comparison with the austerity of 'A Detective's Tale', the plenitude of event and action on display here makes the first film seem even bolder in aesthetic terms.

This analysis will explore the relationship between this film and the previous one, and the construction of the milieu in which both Lynn and Pyall are shown to move. Here I will propose that the interrelation of the episodes through overlapping time schemes produces a self-conscious realism at the level of structure. As we have seen, one aspect of the series that was seen as both its greatest achievement, and most problematic, was its 'realism'. This realism is produced in a range of ways, one of which is structure. The first three films have loose and unpredictable temporal overlaps and some repeated scenes. The connection between the different stories (detective, villain and brief) are not always immediately clear, and it is through the repetitions that the viewer finds their way, understanding that some events are happening simultaneously, in different characters' worlds, rather than sequentially. This portrayal of more than one narrative point of view, and the repetition of scenes with very slight variations to demonstrate this plurality of viewpoint is sophisticated film-making. These are classic modernist strategies, traditionally employed to draw the viewer's attention to the constructedness of the artwork, and to enable them to reflect critically on the way in which its world is being created. Once the same events are shown from different points of view, then the film can be making no simple claim that what it shows is just 'the real', unnarrated. Far from trying to 'trick' viewers into thinking that what they see is real, these films show how the reality that is shown is constructed. This strategy also gives a sense of the 'thickness' of the description of the interlocking milieux of the series, in which there are lots of different stories which occasionally overlap. This in turn intimates that what we are being shown is typical, as well as being particular, and that what we have is a random slice through this underworld. This can be examined in more detail in relation to the opening of this episode, and the treatment of informers.

Realism of structure

The opening of 'A Villain's Tale' matches the opening of 'A Detective's Tale'. In each, the key man is first shown alone, and then working a subordinate informant. Where Pyall met Micky Fielder on the tube, and learned of the whisper that Jack Lynn was 'putting one together', here Jack Lynn sits in a car observing a supermarket and collects a wax key impression from a man in overalls who 'better get back, they'll be wanting to lock up'. In accounts of the casting of the films we have noted the strategy of casting police and criminals from the same pool of actors. This opening rhyme explicitly sets up a comparison between Pyall and Lynn, and the next scene confirms the shared social spaces of police and villains. Here we see Lynn entering a drinking club in the West End, and as he prepares to go upstairs, he meets a man who warns him 'that there are a couple of Old Bill upstairs'. In this warning, Lynn is addressed by name for the first time in the film, and so the identity of the man observing the security lorry is confirmed as Jack Lynn, the villain 'elected' in the previous film.

While the continuity of characters across the two episodes is confirmed, it is not yet clear how the temporality of this tale is related to that of the previous one. However, the device of the comparison between Lynn and Pyall is repeated thirty minutes in, when the temporal relationship between the first two episodes is finally clarified. Here, the rhyme is a cut between two scenes, one with Lynn, one with Pyall, both venting frustration. In the first, Lynn is at home watching the racing, visited by his accomplice for the planned supermarket raid. This is not the enforced domestic daytime television viewing of the unemployed: they discuss business as Jack makes Bob (Steve Ismay) comfortable, drinking spirits with mixers, keeping an eye on the races to see how bets come off, an eye echoed by the camera. Lynn has the concerns of any small businessman, upset at wasted arrangements and expenditure: 'Oh come on Bob, I've gone and got the cars, the shooters, the lock-ups. It all comes to money', but agrees to postpone the job, just as his horse loses, 'That's just about made my day.' The camera in this scene alternates between the television and the men's faces, but here moves into medium close-up on Lynn as he curses, and then there is a sudden cut to a dark exterior scene, followed by a medium close-up on Inspector Pyall in a car.

This scene we have already seen: it is the anticlimax of the previous episode, when the police waited in vain for the Friday raid on the Putney supermarket. Just as Lynn has to work out whether he has been grassed, Pyall wonders if they've been 'tumbled'. He too has incurred expense: the men, the cars, the organisation, the overtime. He curses, 'Sod it.' Both men are frustrated and fed up that the Putney supermarket raid won't take place. The alignment of the two principals through this 'cursing cut' sets them up as adversaries, already in a duel in which they frustrate each other. It also clarifies the time scheme,

Jack Lynn and Bobby Shaw (Steve Ismay) cancel the raid: 'That bastard'

DI Pyall and DS Eric Lethridge (Billy Cornelius) accept they've 'been tumbled': 'Sod it'

showing the audience that the Lynn episode so far has been mainly chronological 'backstory' to the opening Pyall narrative. However, in addition to this narrative structuring, the comparative edit lays out one of the propositions of the series, which is that detectives like Fred Pyall are closer to villains like Jack Lynn than the general public necessarily cares to know.

This imbrication of police and villains, the ecology of the shadowy world in which both move, is the great theme of the piece. As suggested in the analysis of the first film, it is demonstrated most elegantly in the way in which the stories of the informants are treated. For these characters embody the connection of the films' worlds, and appear in both the detective's and the villain's milieux. The elegance of the treatment lies in the fact that it is particularly through the repetition of informer scenes that the overlapping time schemes are tracked. This involves two characters, Micky Fielder and Clifford Harding.

Fielder is an informant from the beginning – it is with him that Pyall's initial rendezvous is kept – and has, by halfway through the second episode been taken out of the action, kneecapped by Lynn. Fielder's home milieu is the second episode, where we see him gathering information in a snooker hall, but he appears in two scenes repeated in the first and second episodes: the opening, initial fingering of Lynn on the tube, discussed in the previous section; and a rather more spectacular scene when Pyall and Fielder meet near a schoolgirl netball game. In this scene, much of the filming is done with Pyall and Fielder on the far side of the netball game, so that the foreground is occupied with adolescent girls in games kit leaping around after the ball. This meeting place is so visually striking, while also so unmotivated by plot, that it requires a little more attention.

In the first film, this colourful and lively scene provides a strong contrast with the grey world of Inspector Pyall, juxtaposing the girls' innocent game with Pyall and Micky's more serious one, while

The repeated meeting between Pyall and Fielder at the netball game

also uniting Fielder and Pyall in their seedy lust, an interpretation ironically acknowledged by Fielder's comment that it would be 'worth getting nicked for'. In the second, when it is repeated, filmed with a very slight shift to Fielder's point of view, its distinctiveness displays the repetition. The scene is so different to everything else that it works as a very recognisable clue for viewers trying to orient themselves in the overlapping time schemes of the films. This netball game, which gives both the viewers and the characters something they can't but look at while their transaction is completed, has nothing to do with the plot and so its inclusion testifies to an ongoing world which pre-exists the drama. It is a guarantee of authenticity: the apparently random inclusion of the real. The repetition of this scene demonstrates that the time scheme is not simply progressive, preparing us for the cut between Lynn and Pyall, and the understanding that from this point on, time proceeds beyond the duration of the 'Detective's Tale'.

The manipulation of Harding in a series of two-hander scenes with Pyall running through three episodes, is one in which the detective gradually implicates him in the case against Lynn. Harding's story is the essential counterpoint to the higher-profile pursuit of the more glamorous Lynn. The false testimony of the ex-con with a family is a decisive blow against Lynn. The intensity of the pressure on Harding in this episode, when, as he puts it, 'I'm not only grassing now, I'm fitting one up', is conveyed through the use of simple close-ups on his face. Harding's vulnerability – his isolation within the image – and, in comparison to Lynn, his lack of affluence and slight physical frame, make him a more wretched victim of Pyall's policing strategy than even Micky Fielder who we last see in a hospital bed. Pyall too is shown in close-up, his face showing no emotion as he points out Harding's limited options. Retrospectively, these close-ups function as barefaced lies, demonstrating that Pyall has acted in consistently bad faith toward Harding, finally forcing him to appear in court to identify Lynn, which is what he promised he wouldn't do. The cost of this act to Harding is shown in the court scene in the next episode when the camera rests for a moment on his face as he blinks when Lynn roars his protest at the lie.

The tiny movement demonstrates the effort behind the testimony, and his recognition that he has breached a moral code.

Harding's collaboration and Micky Fielder's original information are the material from which Inspector Pyall constructs his case. They are his 'irons in the fire', kept warm in case they turn up something helpful, or come in handy. The episodic reappearance of these characters, the repetition of scenes in which they figure and their association with both Pyall and Lynn, demonstrates how this method of policing works at a structural level. The labour of the informant is to mediate between police and criminals, appearing plausible and trustworthy to both. The way in which the informant scenes in the films are organised and repeated, slightly differently emphasised, demonstrates this mediation at a formal level, as well as showing, as a plot detail, how information is transferred and pressure applied.

The villain

When Jack Lynn knocks into a man playing snooker as he leaves a snooker hall early in this episode, he doesn't turn to apologise, and, although the man had been pushed out of the way, he doesn't remonstrate. This interaction, filmed in long shot through the hall, has no attention drawn to it through the cinematography or editing. It 'just happens', naturalistically: someone is in the way as Lynn and two accomplices walk out of the hall. The direction shows us, through the filming of this incident, something of Lynn's status in the snooker hall – his presence had earlier been sufficient to bring a game to a close – but shows it discreetly, intimating stylistically Lynn's own discretion. Lynn is a successful villain because he is careful, and, like Inspector Pyall, pays attention to detail. The first third of this episode follows Lynn as he tries to recruit a team for the Putney supermarket job: this he does systematically, visiting different venues, having a word at an appropriate moment, but always attentive to his surroundings and companions. His quest takes him to all the locations associated with villainy in the crime film: drinking clubs, snooker halls, boxing gyms and bars. And Blair's shooting and editing style presents Lynn's environment as familiar. Characteristically, a scene will open with the camera waiting for the action, rather than cut on movement. There is no neon in the trip to Soho, there are very few exterior or establishing shots. Lynn is at ease and recognised in this world, and it is as if the camera too is patient, just waiting for the right moment and the right man. Although he does drive a cream Jaguar, and dresses well, favouring suede and sheepskin jackets worn with pale polo-neck jerseys, Lynn is not flashy, just comfortable; just like the camera in this world.

As the character name suggests, Lynn is in some ways a 'Jack the Lad', but now mature, a family man with a good standard of living whose wife doesn't work outside the home but 'has a bit of spending money'. He is shown taking his children to school, exchanging racing tips with his milkman, and in bed with his wife. His physical self-confidence is manifested through performance: he moves easily through different spaces, his posture is relaxed and he doesn't raise his voice. The shadow of prison hangs over him throughout this episode though, and there are early indications that his status as a hard man might have repercussions in prison. The first intimation comes early in the episode, when he is recruiting his team, and talks to a man working hard at a punch ball. Bob's punches take up the foreground of the image while he explains that the exercise is a necessity to avoid running to fat 'after all that body-building inside'. The explicit mention of prison provokes Jack into observing 'I heard you did it the easy way', with Bob agreeing, 'Yes sir, no sir, three bags full sir'. The tone of Jack's comment hints that 'the easy way' might not be an honourable option, and Bob's ironic self-description confirms his collusion with authority. So Lynn is shown, in this opening ten minutes, not only to be 'active', but also to be someone who would not serve a prison term 'the easy way'.[60] While the contrast with the morality displayed in the first episode is plain, the full implications of Lynn's code will not become apparent until the last episode.

So the villain of the piece is a respected man – 'nice bloke', says Micky Fielder in the snooker hall – who is careful, discreet and successful. Portraying the villain as a loving family man, in contrast to

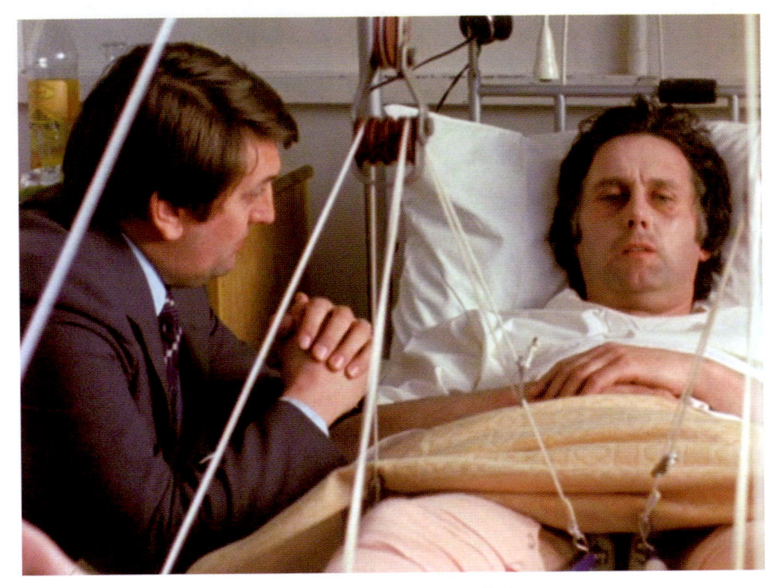

The gravity of Micky Fielder's punishment revealed

the evasive phone conversations Inspector Pyall has with his unseen wife, mobilises sympathy towards Lynn. This is dispatched promptly in the brutal finale to the introduction to Lynn, when he and Bob go round to Micky Fielder's with baseball bats. As Bob says, 'he's got to be hurt'. The hurting is swift, hardly shown, the filming functional, constrained by the dimensions of the small house, no dwelling on damage, only the crack of one knee heard before a swift cut to Inspector Pyall in a hospital corridor. Once again, the link between Pyall and Lynn is made, as Pyall proves himself well able to understand why his informant is strapped up with two smashed kneecaps: 'Well you were a grass, son, got to expect some kind of aggro. Occupational hazard, you could say.'

Romford farce with two gas cookers

Narratively, the Romford job must be shown in some detail in order to make it clear that the police had prior knowledge of a likely job – and chose to employ surveillance – and that Lynn is not involved. This central section of the film is plot-driven, cutting between the many different characters and locations involved, demonstrating the sometimes competitive intricacy of the relationships between different police manors and fiefdoms, the banality of the exercise of power (over snouts, junior officers, car breakers) and the ordinariness of the working days of both policemen and villains. The location shooting follows the progress of the raiders as they move from the favoured generic site of a lockup under a railway viaduct through unremarkable London streets, clogged up with traffic, deploying the device of a surveillant policeman to structure the journey. Cutting between the photographing police officer and the team introduces some tension into the journey, but it also draws the attention of the audience to what is being seen, what is being watched. 'Look at this', 'and this' exhorts the soundtrack of the camera clicking: 'this is evidence'. So this narratively quite complicated section of the film is marked for the audience as involving events and characters that must be marked and remembered.

However, the detail in which the lead-up to the job is shown also reworks familiar tropes of the genre, opening them out, so that instead of the wages raid being exciting, it is much more like the bungled end of a typical day's work. Blair's work in television drama in the 1970s is distinctive in its acceptance of the mess and clutter of everyday life. His is a film-making in which ashtrays get filled and overflow, milk bottles are not always rinsed and beds look as if they've been slept in. These skills in rendering convincing the environment which characters inhabit are here displayed to bring together the team that will do the job. Lynn's comparative success becomes more evident as we witness the home environments of the team his friend John Tully has got together: council flats, full ashtrays, eating breakfast standing up.

Again, the provision of mundane detail, such as a mother worrying that her son will eat all the bacon, has no bearing on the plot, but functions instead to show these men who make a living as armed robbers as ordinary, with wives and mothers. It is after this context has been established, and just before the men rush the gas board wages van, that the film secures its evidence by cutting to Lynn and Cathy (Deirdre Costello) in bed. The more languorous pace of this scene, the closer focus, the lack of extraneous detail all demonstrate that Lynn is in a quite different place to Romford. But here of course, in the Lynns' intimate space, there is no police photographer to record the evidence.

The raid itself is most like 'the squealing tyres' of *The Sweeney* which was attracting enormous audiences in the mid-1970s. All the ingredients are there: the tip-off, the CID detectives in unmarked cars, the masks, guns and shouting, the security men, the screaming women, the getaway van and the car chase. Here, as with the scene when Lynn and Bob force their way into the house to kneecap Micky Fielder, the constraints of location shooting are exploited to enhance the sense of panic, confusion and force. Camera movement is inhibited inside the gas board building, movement is too close to make sense of, parts of people obscure the view and the soundtrack is indecipherable with shouting. The intensity of the action is overwhelming, if brief. However as there is a farcical doubling of gas cookers in the plot and a great deal of incompetence, the raid is most un-*Sweeney*-esque. For a raid on the gas board, the robbers choose to use an old gas stove as a battering ram. Their arrival coincides with that of a couple of policemen coming to pick up a new gas stove for their chief's wife. The banal venality of the senior policeman is matched with the high anxiety of the gang as they wait for the arrival of the wages van. Far from being a tale in which clever coppers outwit intrepid robbers, two sets of men carrying gas stoves pretty much crash into each other by accident.

In the final part of the film, the initiative returns to Fred Pyall, and we watch him construct the case against Jack Lynn. Pyall's actions here repeat many of those shown in the first episode: conversations with colleagues, dawn raids, interrogation of suspects, discovery of weapons. He is out and about, busy in his work, calling in favours, offering advice, ensuring consistency in the police diaries ('their diaries won't have gone in yet'), and showing enterprise in securing what he needs, which his boss has indicated to him must be a civilian witness and some 'good forensic'.

The bungled raid with gas cookers

And Jack Lynn too knows what Pyall needs: 'You've got one on the books and I'm the body.' The initial conversation we see between Pyall and Lynn demonstrates a shared understanding about habitual procedure in these cases. And it is in this conversation that the first intimation is given that it is Lynn's innocence which will prove his undoing; he himself proposes that the first thing he would have done had he been on the Romford raid would be to offer Pyall a cut of the proceeds. Lynn's innocence, with an alibi provided by his wife, makes him less able to defend himself from an enterprising CID man, and Pyall is shown to be enterprising, determined and systematic in gathering the necessary evidence. He is shown making up the proof that Lynn was on the job: gathering and falsifying forensic evidence, coaching witnesses and minimising evidence of a police cock-up. And in this careful establishment of the authenticity of his false case, the film offers another way of reflecting on realism and believing the evidence of what we see. If the earlier sequence with the police surveillance officer photographing the raid proposed one way of thinking about visible evidence, Inspector Pyall's creativity offers another. It is Inspector Pyall who interprets the blurred photographs as 'giving us more scope', and it is this scope which he exploits to frame Lynn. So in this final part of the episode, before Lynn goes before the magistrate, we see Pyall working like a film director to tell a story, checking that all the constituent elements are in play – even having to write the script for Clifford Harding, one of the actors – as well as dealing with significant details about props. The film shows us the painstaking detail of the *mise en scène* of a conviction.

A Brief's Tale

The third film marks an institutional shift from the underworld to the 'above ground' of the legal system and the courts, opening with Ken Campbell emerging from a black cab to enter an office labelled 'Alex Gladwell, Solicitor' on a busy street corner. Gladwell, the most Dickensian of the characters in the drama, partly because of Ken

Alex Gladwell (Ken Campbell) arrives at work by taxi

Campbell's performance, is already familiar from the previous episodes. Pyall has described him as 'a little bald-headed bloke … flapping about like a demented penguin' and we have already seen Pyall both avoid his phone calls, and be collegially familiar when they do talk. It is clear that Gladwell and Pyall are familiar to each other. One of the achievements of *Law and Order* is its depiction of the banality of the corruption it anatomises. In Les Blair's resolutely deadpan filming and editing, the series of little deals which greases the underside of the armed robbery court case in which Jack Lynn is framed is shown as quite unexceptional to all participants. So commonplace are the transactions that many conversations are conducted in tones of unmarked irony, as when Fred Pyall informs Gladwell that he would be 'outraged' to learn that some charges against Lynn would be dropped. The completely expressionless delivery of this line displays their mutual understanding of the game. Thus the theatre of the courtroom, which occupies most of the episode's screen time – the spatial disposition of protagonists at different levels, the judge's robes, the barristers' wigs, the evidentiary exhibits, the ritual of procedure – is produced as a performance in which lines have been distributed and learned elsewhere. In this theatre only the jury and Jack Lynn 'act naturally'. The exceptions to this deadpan treatment of the action – mainly medium shots, movement in frame but little camera mobility, many images framed in a naturalistically 'messy' manner – are the shots of Jack Lynn which sparsely punctuate the episode. These function as reaction shots, so that despite being 'A Brief's Tale', with its structure based on the solicitor's practice of Alex Gladwell, Jack Lynn is identified as the character to whom the narrative is happening.

Gladwell's working day, like those of each of the other protagonists, is shown to consist of a series of meetings. He has to take on new clients, investigate possible clients, attend cases in progress, agree strategies and, like each of the other protagonists, constantly monitor the progress of his interests. In the opening scene, the grimy location of Gladwell's office and the London accent of his secretary lay the ground for the later comparison between the slightly seedy solicitor and the evidently expensive, confidently upper-middle-class barrister whom he instructs to act for Lynn. Gladwell's busy-ness is an impression partly created through Campbell's performance so that he seems to be scurrying between appointments, but also by sharp editing between the locations of his different enterprises. The taxi opening is predictive: Gladwell is not a man with the time for public transport, and is constantly arriving in, and leaving, scenes. The brevity of some of his appearances, the sense given of a man always on the move, offers a comparison with Pyall. Each man spends his working day checking the status of his enterprises, but while Pyall is deliberate, patient and expressionless, Gladwell is animated and mobile. In this episode, we follow Gladwell's involvement with Lynn from his engagement by Lynn's wife through to the aftermath of the verdict, but we also see a range of other work, from a magistrate's court defence of fraud to advising a police officer accused of corruption. This situates the Lynn case as one of many for Gladwell, and not in any way exceptional. Campbell was best known as a theatrical performer of bravura originality, and Garnett describes 'Ken's previous work' as 'large', observing that 'he had to compress himself down into this character'. This 'compression', which Campbell describes as the result of 'taking instruction in not-acting', gives his character an intensity and nervous energy that enhances a sense of his continual focus on the next deal.[61]

The role of a solicitor in the British legal system is to advise a client on the different possibilities available to them under the law. In particular, it is often the role of the solicitor to point out that there may be a divergence between the law of the land and what the client perceives as natural justice, and to introduce ideas such as strategic pleading. The solicitor is often the bearer of the news that the law is an institutional system in which adversarial performance and legal precedent can determine outcomes. As Gladwell puts it to Lynn in their first meeting: 'That's like saying that just because you're innocent, the jury is automatically going to return a verdict of not guilty.' It is the solicitor who is the broker between the client and his advocate in court, the barrister, and it is the solicitor's professional expertise which is instrumental in assessing the strategic emphasis of a case. This expertise, this understanding that the law is a system with its own rhetoric, can make the advice of a solicitor seem very cynical, as when, in this episode, Gladwell proposes to a client that 'we'll make you a victim of circumstance, that's what the magistrate will want to hear'. The sense of the law as performance is made more palpable here because of the intensity of the way in which Campbell's 'non-acting' is also a performance. The brief's tale is a tale of mediation. Gladwell is shown to move between worlds, to break bread with a wide range of contacts, with a versatility which allows him to be comfortable consuming whisky and ginger, tea and a Danish, or a red wine he can identify as being from Piedmont and 'a bit like Barolo'. Of Inspector Pyall he uses the term 'certainly accessible' to indicate the possibility of bribery; he is himself shown to be extremely adaptable, a tenacious professional who can deal with men both above and below him socially.

Gladwell is shown to scent the possibility of money in Lynn's case at the very moment at which he denies it, 'Mrs Lynn, that is not a consideration.' He takes money from Lynn for both legal and illegal purposes. The barrister he recommends is expensive, but so too is the bribe offered to the CID. The scale of the legitimate legal expense, which will be covered by the 'nice few quid' Lynn has tucked away, signals that Lynn can also be pumped for illegal payments to the police. However, in one of several double-binds for Lynn, the very availability of these funds demonstrates to Pyall the justice of pursuing him. Gladwell does turn up evidence of police pressure on witnesses, but this again does not play in Lynn's favour in court. The lawyers then extort a further round of payment from Lynn by suggesting that he pursue the police for malicious prosecution, which, again, turns out to be strategically disastrous for Lynn, but, as the barrister puts it to Gladwell, keeps Lynn's 'proceeds in circulation'. Thus with a certain black humour, the moral economy of the programme (Lynn is, in a larger frame, guilty) is supported by a radical redistributive project, in which his ill-gotten gains are made to re-enter the system of law and order.

Lynn is shown to be the victim of a miscarriage of justice. What I want to explore in the analysis of this episode is whether this is laboured too much. This is not a point about whether or not judges like Mr Justice Quigley (André Van Gyseghem) serve in the High Court. It is clear, from the history of miscarriage of justice in the UK that the judiciary have frequently been inclined to believe the police and expert witnesses over the testimony of the accused. The popular image of the judge out of touch with the reality of everyone else in court is also well established in British culture, and nicely handled here in a little detail about the use of Fairy Liquid Squeezy washing-up liquid bottles to spray ammonia, in which the judge must ask, 'What are Squeezy tubs?'. So it is not a referential question about whether it is likely, or true, that judges behave as Quigley does, repeatedly dismissing evidence which impugns the police and damages the prosecution case, then adducing these suggestions to Lynn's guilt. Nor is it a question about whether different judges are known to have different proclivities, and that lawyers will assess the chances of their clients on these grounds. Nor is it about whether police officers collude with each other to strengthen their case –

'What are Squeezy tubs?'

or indeed about any of the 'underside' activities that we have been shown in previous episodes. It is instead an aesthetic question about whether the episode, in its project to expose the corruption of the system, weights its own side too heavily, particularly through the choices about how to represent the judge.

The structuring paradox of the episode, and one which prepares the viewer for Lynn's transformation into a more tragic hero in the final part, is that Lynn's innocence here is his downfall. He is a villain, and this both he and others acknowledge, but he was really not involved in this case of the robbery at the Romford gas board. However, his alibi, that he was in bed with his wife, although true, is almost comic in its strategic inappropriateness. His innocence renders him vulnerable to the blandishments and false optimism of Gladwell, and thus he cannot play the game. Despite his knowledge of the system, and his recognition of the significance of Quigley's reputation, 'That slag, I've got no chance', Jack persists in asserting his particular, circumstantial innocence. His frequent outbursts in court are the eruption of the unscripted into an environment where all else is scripted, except the verdict. So Lynn is shown to provoke the judge into what we surmise will be harsher sentencing by his very inability to control his innocent outrage. His innocence, ironically, prevents him negotiating a better deal. Here the series offers an anatomy of the gains and losses of this pattern of policing. For Lynn is shown to have made a good living from armed robbery for many years. This is demonstrated forcibly when Gladwell first visits him to prepare the case, and Lynn is wearing an expensive suede jacket and good-quality polo-neck jersey: even held in custody, he is a well-dressed man. The particularity of this fit-up is, then, by implication, set against its preventative and punitive value.

Here comes the judge

The police crime series typically ends with the capture, rather than the trial or imprisonment, of a wrongdoer. The simple opposition between police and thieves, right and wrong, is more exciting than the long, undramatic and often obscure processes of the law. 'A Brief's Tale' takes the series out of the territory of the police series, and into the more complex issue of institutional politics. It marks a shift both in its attention to the modalities of power, and the power relationships within the fictional world. Lynn, virile, attractive and successful, is in his own words, here the victim of a stitch-up, and the viewer begins to suspect that he is no match for the many-layered institutional corruption and establishment myopia. However I think it arguable that as the case is made using belt and braces (the corrupt deals and the stubbornly pro-police judge), the type of attention demanded of the viewer becomes less discriminating. Instead of having to work our way through what is shown in order to come to judgment ourselves, we are more explicitly shown what to think.

Mr Justice Quigley is set up from the beginning of the episode as a judge who will be unsympathetic to Lynn's case. When DI Pyall and DS Lethridge (Billy Cornelius) are discussing the chances of Lynn's case in the pub, Pyall counsels optimism about the outcome, once again using the irony which characterises many of the interactions in the serial: 'If we can get it before the right kind of judge – someone like Quigley – who won't even tolerate the idea of a fit-up ... he knows the police don't do that kind of thing'. Pyall's view of Quigley is swiftly endorsed by both the barrister, Horace McMillan (Michael Griffiths), and by Lynn. McMillan informs Lynn of the identity of the judge, framing his information as 'some bad news', and goes on to describe Quigley as 'biased in favour of the police'. Lynn, less temperately, exclaims 'not that wicked bastard – I've got no chance'. So before the trial has even started, Lynn sees that he had 'been done up like a bloody kipper', and initially refuses to even appear in court before the judge, who is played as a stubborn, pompous, elderly establishment figure, quick to dismiss any aspersions cast on police evidence and to read these suggestions as signs of moral cowardice on Lynn's part. As viewers who have followed the drama so far, we know that Lynn is being set up. We have followed the decisions and deals that have led to his appearance at the Old Bailey charged with a farcical robbery which he did not commit. So not only is Lynn the most attractive figure in the drama, but we fully understand the extent to which he is here 'a victim of circumstance'. This is exquisitely shown in a sequence about the balaclava masks worn by the alleged gang in the robbery. The balaclava delivers an image which condenses the fit-up, underlining Lynn's innocence, and this sequence forms the climax of the trial before the suspense of the delayed verdict. We have already seen, in the previous episode, Pyall take hair from Lynn's comb and plant it inside the balaclava held in the evidence bag in the police store. So we already know that Gladwell is right to ask 'Is it?' to Pyall's comment that 'Evidence is evidence.' However, in the court, the evidence of the balaclava with 'forensic' is produced. This sequence is given in some detail, with the camera cutting between barrister, jury, judge and the book of photographic evidence, so that the lawyer's point is laid out for judge, jury and viewer. The photographs of the raid show the robbers wearing balaclavas, which makes identification both difficult and – as Inspector Pyall had been quick to note – flexible.

Jack Lynn tries on the balaclava mask

Lynn's lawyer requests that he try on the balaclava in the dock. He stands up in the dock and struggles to get the black knitted mask over his head. It is far too small, and doesn't cover his face or head, with the eyeholes pulled gaping wide up on his forehead. A ripple of laughter is heard in the court: the mask so obviously doesn't fit.

And there Lynn stands, unable to see, a ludicrous spectacle of a big strong man with a woolly black mask covering part of his head. For a moment, it seems things may go Lynn's way as Pyall's attention to detail has been insufficient, and the result is funny: there is a cut to the jury laughing. Mr Justice Quigley, however, sees things differently, and finally, after an interrogation of Pyall about the forensic and identification evidence, the camera returns to Lynn, who, it becomes clear, has been standing in the dock with the mask half on throughout the sequence, 'done up like a bloody kipper', his impotence reflected in his inability to portray more than a non-speaking part in the form of 'evidence', and he is given permission to take off the mask. After he sits back down, Lynn gets a comb from his pocket and combs his hair. This little gesture, this little vanity, which gives an indication of Lynn's sense of himself, rhymes with the same act made when the police raided his house to take him into custody which then, disastrously, gave Pyall the source of the hair combings which he planted. Lynn is shown to be a man who minds what he looks like, and the drama poses the question of whether having been made to look a fool in court, standing to be laughed at in the mask, will prove sufficient to get him off.

However, the judge's disregard for what he is told is in a way preposterous. We have had laid out for us very carefully the photographic evidence that is also seen by the jury, and the mask and the man are different. The judge is shown to be outrageously biased in favour of the police, and this is so outrageous that, in concert with our knowledge of Lynn's innocence, he can seem, if not perverse, unbelievable. In terms of the moral and dramatic economy of the film, Quigley does not need to be this biased to secure an unjust conviction for Lynn. The fact that judges of this type existed is not the point. Nor does it affect my argument that the contemporary cases of George Davis and George Ince, in both of which there was extremely problematic identification evidence, may well have strengthened the film-makers' determination to depict a judge behaving in this way. The point is that the drama, with its upper-class 'wicked bastard' judge pre-empts imaginative involvement by the viewer. As Jason Jacobs observed of the political message of a much later television drama, *Casualty*, 'Meaning is not made available to be discovered in the interrelationship of event and viewpoint. The responsibility for meaning is held entirely within the presentation: we are shown how to feel.'[62]

The particular consequence here, given that the jury acquits those we know to be guilty, and convicts the innocent Lynn, is that the jury, despite the suspense created through their failure to reach a unanimous verdict, seems stupid. The dramatic structure is such that we have understood what is behind the courtroom appearance throughout the film. The audience knows the truth throughout. This, in combination with the provocation of the judge's repeated dismissal of what we know to be true about police collusion, puts the audience in a position of such superiority over the jurors that it is difficult to imagine how it seems to them, neither are we encouraged to. They are represented without much attention except for the moment when they are shown to laugh at Lynn in the ill-fitting hat. Their verdict seems incomprehensible and perverse. So paradoxically, we are aligned with Fred Pyall's puzzlement about the jury's verdict, as he ponders on the acquittal of the guilty: 'Makes you wonder though, it's not enough to get them banged to rights.'

The dramatic advantage of Mr Justice Quigley's unshakeable faith in the police though, lies in the way in which the episode can be concluded. This final sequence is the judgment of the film on the events depicted. After sentencing Lynn, Quigley chooses to address the court over the question of the allusions that have been made about police conduct. Much of this speech runs as soundtrack over the image of Pyall and Lethridge standing, impassive, as they listen to the judge's commendation of 'the integrity, diligence and the scrupulous manner in which they have conducted themselves'. Throughout the play, characters such as Pyall and Gladwell have adopted the language of the law with unmarked irony as they negotiate their way through its constraints. Here, the judge's sincerely meant commendation functions ironically as the soundtrack to the image of the policemen, and so sound and image together suggest the hypocrisy of the British establishment.

A Prisoner's Tale

You're supposed to be a hard boy – you should be able to take it.

Stephen Collins (P. H. Moriarty) to Lynn in *A Prisoner's Tale*

Keep your nose clean, bide your time, do your porridge.

Fletcher (Ronnie Barker) in 'New Faces, Old Hands', ep.1 *Porridge* (1974)

In 2008, when *Law and Order* was released on DVD, the cover design featured photofit likenesses of each of the three central protagonists, Fred Pyall, Jack Lynn and Alex Gladwell (taken from an original *Radio Times* feature) with the question 'Detective, criminal, lawyer, who should be the prisoner?'[63] The structure of the series proposed in this design is thus 3+1, with the first three individually focused episodes, each, in their way, a 'day' in the life of their named protagonist, while the final episode is, to co-opt the terminology of the series, the 'result'. By the time the viewer gets to the final instalment of *Law and Order*, there is no ambiguity about who the prisoner is, but the DVD cover does point to the way in which the final film is differently placed to the others. In the first three, the viewer was tracing the overlaps between different worlds, coming to understand the similar ways in which detective, villain and solicitor were all involved in business: the business of law, order and villainy. The final episode takes place almost exclusively in the total institution of prison, and traces the breaking of Jack Lynn.

I have suggested that the earlier episodes gained depth and plausibility through their interlocking time schemes, which demonstrated at a formal level the interconnections that were being proposed between protagonists and institutions. This episode has none of these overlapping time schemes. Instead, the confinement of prison is produced for the viewer, as well as Jack Lynn, through the unrelenting focus within the walls of the prison, including, during Jack's escape attempt, detailed close-ups of the fences, barbed wire, security cameras and actual walls which render the prison 'high security'. It was in the prison filming that Blair found one of his 'rules' about the production most testing. In addition to the decision not to include music, he had also determined, right at the beginning, that he would never put the camera in a position that wasn't 'human':

> for example, they used to do it a lot in those days, if they were filming in a cell, they'd put the camera on the ceiling, and look down, and I just said I'm not going to do that, and then we got to Kilmainin, and I saw all these cells and I thought, why the hell did I make this rule and what am I going to do now? Basically there's two positions for the camera, one at each end of the cell.[64]

The result of Blair's observation of these constraints in the ambition to 'make it real', which is done with considerable imagination, does produce an apprehension of imprisonment for the viewer. The director's 'rule' produces a sense of formal constraint, of literally being cramped, which evokes Lynn's condition.

Three characters from previous episodes penetrate the prison: the solicitor Alex Gladwell, Cathy Lynn, and Inspector Chatt from A10, who takes the details of Jack's complaint against the police. Of these, only Cathy appears more than once, and it is she, at the end of the episode, who is shown in the only scene outside the prison, seeking the help of her MP. So the sense of a whole social world created by the first three episodes here shrinks right down to a single institution and the hierarchies and survival strategies within it. Time becomes singular and sequential, twenty years to be counted in days: twenty-eight days in 'chokey', one hundred and eighty days loss of remission, fifty-six days 'as an exemplary prisoner'. Lynn's eventual defeat is demonstrated by a shot of him hunched in a cell, trying hard to retain his sanity by counting not days, but the number of bricks in the wall. Here, the viewer's world too is shrunk, as subjective camera is used in close-up, jerking from brick to identical brick.

The episode again has a loose tripartite structure. The first and longest part (forty-five minutes) chronicles the initial part of Lynn's sentence, when he is arranging and awaiting the result of his appeal, and thus in denial about his prison term. The second part, after the cruelly imparted news that his appeal (for which he sold his house) has resulted in a reduction of his sentence by only three years ('I have some very good news for you'), chronicles active resistance: bribing prison officers to permit a conjugal visit and involvement in escape schemes. In this part, the conventions of the prison film are most apparent, including concealed tools and knotted sheets, but the viewer is disappointed to see Jack caught hanging on the barbed wire, his hands bleeding as he shouts, in the intimation of his final defeat, 'for Christ's sake get me down'. The final and shortest part documents the breaking of Lynn, and the film finishes with a brief coda in the prison grounds.

It has already been intimated, in episode two, that Jack considers resistance to authority to be the proper behaviour of the hard man in prison, and this hard man has been given twenty years for a crime that he did not commit. He is shown to put this into practice in the opening scene, in which he stands before the prison doctor's desk, with his trousers dropped, answering questions such as whether he has VD, lice or crabs, and whether he is depressed at his sentence. On being declared 'fit to work', and told that he can get dressed, he instead urinates in the direction of the desk. This is filmed so that the viewer is initially as surprised as Dr Eynshaw (Harry Walker). The scene uses a classical shot/reverse-shot set-up, alternating between a view of the doctor at his desk, looking up at Lynn, and a head-and-shoulders shot of Lynn, looking down at the doctor. From the shots of Lynn, it looks as if he is fully dressed. It is only from the shots of the doctor, in which part of Lynn's naked thigh is visible, in combination with the doctor's

Jack Lynn's early triumph in catching the prison authorities by surprise

questions, that the viewer has been able to deduce that Lynn is standing with his trousers dropped. When given permission to get dressed, his shoulder movements, in the head-and-shoulders shot, could, for a moment, be interpreted as part of dressing, but then we cut back to the view of the doctor, with Lynn's thigh in the foreground, and the arc of liquid. The doctor does not look up until alerted by the sound of the urine. A close-up of Lynn's face in the hubbub shows him give a little smile: the satisfaction of causing trouble, in this case the short-term strategic advantage of catching the enemy off guard by declaring hostilities early.

It is after this scene, when Lynn is shown being put into a cell alone, 'you're on report', that the episode title comes up. This clever opening manages to introduce new viewers to the set-up as well as develop themes from previous episodes, while the second scene, with the episode title, functions more like an establishing shot, presenting a clearly identifiable prison setting with a cell, institutional paint and a barred window. Lynn's answer to the query about depression, 'how would you feel if you'd been fitted up by the police' condenses the narrative so far, while his provocation hints at what will follow, as does his vehement rejection of the offered 'something to help you sleep'.

The economy of this opening, in which nothing is wasted, does more than introduce new viewers, and remind committed viewers about what has happened. For it also demonstrates the way in which this episode will handle questions of genre and realism, while introducing a suitably resistant hero. The knowledge about setting, character and narrative that this scene offers can be given so economically because of the deep generic familiarity of the set-up of the prison film. Truculent, unjustly sentenced prisoners, brutal guards and prison doctors are familiar figures from both film and television. And as prisons are closed institutions, it is on these images that most people's ideas of what a prison is like are based (even if what they think is that prisons can't be like they are shown in movies). So the hint of this setting is sufficient to set in motion possible narrative events (a spell in solitary confinement; a confrontation with the governor; an escape attempt), as well as the expectation of likely characters (the established prison hard man, a sympathetic warder, a sadistic warder) and tropes (clanging doors, concealed weapons). This opening, then, both invokes these generic expectations, but also hints at how they will be treated. The camerawork and editing is both cleverly planned and undeclarative. In the medical examination of new prisoner Lynn, this happened, it says. The doctor's expostulation, 'you're a maniac', and Lynn's little smile, show the emotions at stake, but there is no recourse to zoom or extreme close-up for emphasis.

The scene is not just austere though: it is also excessive, in that a prisoner urinates in an office. This early introduction to bodily waste – the arc of liquid shown quite clearly – points to one of the strategies that is engaged in this film to convince viewers of its verisimilitude. Lynn here is resorting to one of the few expressive resources of the prisoner, and while we are rather blasé about vomit, excrement and bodily fluids on twenty-first-century television, it is worth noting how very shocking this prison – where people have to fish about in pots of sloppy waste searching for keys – is in a broadcast environment in which the familiar representation of prison is the situation comedy *Porridge*. *Porridge*'s comparatively palatial set, which permits camera set-ups horizontal to the cell's length, is more likely to feature concealed alcohol in the bedframe than the smelly, splashy business of 'slopping out'.

The spatial and physical constraints of the prison, and the ingenuity of the location filming in evoking the feel and culture of the prison, are demonstrated vividly in the 'slopping-out' sequence halfway through the film when Jack is still hopeful about his appeal. The scene, demonstrating the importance of sound to this film, opens with the shouted reports of warders on each floor that all prisoners are present in their cells, 'thirty-three on the twos, Sir', 'thirty-four on the threes, Sir', showing the prison as a panopticon with the sightlines co-ordinated to monitor the inmates. The familiar structure of a British Victorian prison, with the cells on several floors ranged round an open central area, traversed by staircases and walkways, serves to give a sense of both the ritualised control, and the volatility, of this mass of men. The scene features one long shot (fifty-nine seconds) to trace Lynn's movement from his cell, carrying his plastic pot, to the sluice where it can be emptied. In this shot, in which all prisoners shown are carrying either full or empty pots and jugs, the camera pans slowly from a position near the sluice tracing Jack's progress along the landing. The simplicity of the camera movement is counterpointed by the range of other movement within the shot: the greeting of Bobby Mark; a prisoner from the landing on the other side trying to dash across to a shorter queue; a prisoner catching something thrown from a higher landing; a discussion with a prison officer, then with another inmate and finally, much closer up, standing in the queue with its goodnatured chat.

This long shot, which is lent visual interest through the use of movement from above and in front of Jack's progress along the landing

The long 'slopping-out' shot

which is its focus, matches the routine of the daily activity depicted with its steady, undemonstrative gaze. It catches the variety of little interactions in this highly controlled environment, but it also recruits the viewer into the constant surveillance about which Jack complains repeatedly. For we are here watching men queue to dispose of their excretions, and the unpleasantness of the task is made clear through the attempts of two prisoners to jump queues.

If the third film was dominated by different kinds of evidence and testimony, and recurrent matters of vision were caught up with questions of identification, record, truth and memory, then in this episode the matters of vision are articulated through questions of surveillance, voyeurism, hiding and seeking. The burden of punishment is shown to be, not so much confinement – although of course it is that, but the exposure of every crevice of the body to a punitive gaze. Prison officers exercise their power through their right to look, and their decisions, at certain times, to neither look nor hear. Prisoners are always vulnerable to being looked at, and are often unable themselves to see, dependent instead on sound and noise to understand what is happening outside their own cells. This, as I have discussed in the slopping-out sequence, puts the viewer in a slightly different position to that solicited in the previous three films. For we too are watching the prisoners, and watching the prison officers wake sleeping prisoners, search through family photographs and spy on attempts at 'conjugals'.

Jack Lynn's role as a narrative agent has gradually reduced throughout the series from his rumoured activity in the first film, through planning the Putney raid in the second. By the end of that film, he was in detention. By the end of the third, sentenced. In this final one, imprisoned, he is able to initiate little. The scale of the observation in the filming also changes, so that there is a rendering of details which in the wider world might be insignificant, but here are the stuff and currency of everyday life. In the mailbag workshop, there is a blackboard on which is chalked the number of prisoners in the room at any one time. When Lynn leaves the room for an unexpected visit, we are shown the gesture, involving the least possible effort by the supervising prison officer, through which the '10' is changed to a '9': he rubs out only the '1', and adds a tail to the '0'. There are close-ups of cell walls, of food and of Jack's hands as he sews mailbags; the viewer is offered a double vision in which the significance of the detail resonates with both prisoner's and gaoler's eye.

Apart from Lynn, the most significant figure in this episode is the prisoner Bobby Mark, already mentioned in the discussion of A10 in Chapter 1. Mark is important in two ways to the structure of this film. First, Lynn's fate in prison is anticipated by the overheard and glimpsed brutal treatment of Mark. It is made clear from the beginning of the episode that there will be a battle of wills between Lynn and the prison governor. Indeed, after first meeting Lynn, Governor Maudling (Edward Cast) observes that he doesn't want him disrupting 'his prison', saying that 'he'd rather have him transferred to Broadmoor'. The implications of this comment about Broadmoor (the prison for the criminally insane) do not become clear until much later in the episode, when Lynn is

Bobby Mark (Bruce White) at the beginning of 'A Prisoner's Tale'

Jack Lynn near the end of 'A Prisoner's Tale'

forcibly injected with a tranquilliser, just as we had seen with Bobby Mark in the opening. The forcible injections are shown to be the decisive factor in breaking Lynn ('I can play this game as long as you'), in the context of a brutal regime of solitary confinement for fifty-six days which restarts at any sign of insubordination. Thus the opening comment about Broadmoor can be understood as the granting of permission to the prison officers to behave as they find necessary to break Lynn, even if it involves permanent mental damage, or the inducement of the appearance of such.

Mark's condition is partly explained as a consequence of his time in prison and he who seems so different to Lynn at the beginning of the film functions, by the time of his death, as a harbinger of the destiny that awaits Lynn. Mark's other role, though, is to demonstrate Lynn's decency, which is a pre-requisite for the realignment of his fate as tragic. Just as it was Lynn's innocence that ensured his conviction in the third film, in the final one, it is Lynn's complaints on Mark's behalf, which start on his first night, which lead him into further conflict with the authorities. The concern for Mark, which is very believably shown by Peter Dean, particularly when he watches Bobby, with great difficulty, sign his name to a letter written for him, and the various actions he takes on his part, reveal Lynn as a man with a moral sense and the proper obligation of the strong to protect the weak. It is an equivalent to the sequence in which Lynn takes his daughters to school in episode two, and represents the thread through which Lynn's transition to a more tragic figure, for whom we are asked to feel pity, is achieved.

The inhumanity of prisons and their failings as a form of punishment are topics that recur in Newman's work, as do processes of accommodation to internal power structures and gradual institutionalisation. The 1991 three-part drama, *For the Greater Good* has an initiating HIV-in-prisons story, and, like *Law and Order*, shows a concerned MP pessimistic about his powers to affect anything. There are moment in this episode when an explicitly campaigning authorial voice becomes audible, particularly in Lynn's speech to a disciplinary inquiry committee, when, after first admitting that he was in the wrong to attack a supervisor, he makes a plea to be given a chance to serve his term with 'self-respect and dignity'. This scene shows Lynn as a decent man, able to admit he was at fault to lash out, but also able to mobilise his intelligence and experience to ask for fair treatment. However, just as the magistrates in episode two, and the judge in episode three, were shown to be completely out of touch with the reality of policing, so here, the committee members are shown to be naively trusting about the nature of the regime – as well as, of course, keen to catch the train home. So the moment of Lynn's greatest maturity, in which he makes a general case about how a penal system could work is shown to be more ineffectual than a later smuggled letter.

Most of this film is shot inside. In the several exercise-yard scenes, the camera never moves upward, so we never see the sky, which appears for the first time as night background to a security camera monitoring the prison walls during Jack's escape attempt. In this context, with prisoners confined to cells, and the camera confined to walkways and corridors and offices, there is a moment of relief when, towards the end of the film, Cathy Lynn is shown outside in the London streets, looking for the office of her MP. Although there is still no sky, the visual detail of the rather down-at-heel street image, in comparison to the austerity of the prison images, emphasises the sensual deprivation of the film's main environment. This is the only moment in the four films where a female character is shown to act alone, and the only scene in this film set outside the prison. It is also though, another moment of authorial explanation, as the MP at the Camden Labour Centre, surrounded by political posters, explains his familiarity with the sedation of prisoners and that the drug is 'the same as one used in mental hospitals' (i.e. probably Largactil, although the drug is never named), but also confesses his relative impotence. This scene seeks to bring Jack Lynn's plight out of the closed world of the prison, and locate it within a more familiar world of parliamentary politics. It also marks a direct nod to the contemporary case of the convicted bullion robber, George Ince who was sedated with Largactil in prison, as the heavy framed glasses of the MP, played by Harry Landis, make him look very like Ian Mikardo, the MP most active in this case.[65] This welcome brief excursion into the real world provides an explanatory caesura, after which the film returns to the most brutal treatment of Lynn.

One of the structural difficulties of long-form drama is the concluding of a fully realised world in which viewers have invested time and imaginative sympathy. Sentencing the central character to twenty years in prison is a brutal solution, as it literally takes him out of the created social world and shuts him away inside one marked by monotony and repetition. However, it has its costs, as the drive to closure, which is here presented through the relentless subjugation of Lynn, and the stripping away of his character, so that there really is nothing left to say, can make a final episode very unrelenting. This reduction in range in this film, in which Lynn receives nothing but bad treatment in prison, in my view oversimplifies the analysis, permitting one to think that prisons are as they are because only evil people work

The prison officer's smile (Farrell Sheridan as Principal Officer McClean)

there. This oversimplification is condensed, very near the end of the film, in the image of Principal Officer McClean (Farrell Sheridan) smirking in the background as the prison governor informs Lynn that an inquiry has upheld a suicide verdict on the death of Bobby Mark. Again, as I argued in relation to Judge Quigley in episode three, this is not a point about whether or not some prison officers might, in equivalent circumstances, express vindictive pleasure. Nor is it to dispute the basic proposition of the last episode, that discipline in prisons is partly maintained through the 'breaking' of particularly recalcitrant prisoners. It is a point about dramatic complexity: this is a moment when the film 'insists' on the unequivocal malevolence of prison officers, and thus unwittingly plays into the hands of its critics. This smirk undermines the richness of the structural analysis of the interlocking institutional worlds of crime and punishment in the series as a whole. It is a bit like Jack Lynn pissing on the prison doctor's desk at the beginning of the film. Lynn gains a moment's satisfaction in this opening skirmish; the prison officer is shown to be 'an evil bastard'. But Jack loses the war, and no understanding is achieved if it is all just down to evil bastards.

Tony Garnett, in pre-broadcast publicity for the series, discussed what he characterised as the 'the most difficult case for the liberals', 'the intelligent, dedicated criminal', of which Jack Lynn is an example. Garnett continues, '[t]he attitude the audience may have about the detective is not going to be reinforced by us being sympathetic to criminals … . It really is left-wing infantilism to get sentimental about crooks'.[66] While *Law and Order* never hesitates in its depiction of Lynn as an experienced and successful armed robber, my analysis shows that the attitude to Lynn is more complex than Garnett suggests.

In the various comparisons between Lynn and Pyall made in the first two films, Lynn is the more sympathetic character. He is an attractive man, well dressed and well respected; a happily married man who still has sex with his wife while also being a loving father. Pyall, in contrast, lives a more monochromatic and seedy life, picking up women and lying to his wife. Peter Dean's performance gives Lynn both presence and authority, particularly in contrast to other criminal characters such as Harding and Shaw. We do see Lynn kneecap Pyall's informant, so we are shown, unsentimentally, his violence. However, as the narrative hangs on the fact that Lynn, although 'a villain', and planning a raid, was not actually on the raid for which he is convicted, we do not see him conducting an armed robbery and instead watch him convicted by a system in which his innocence works against him. The injustice of Lynn's treatment in the third film, which pivots on the 'balaclava' moment and what I have argued to be the dramatically unnecessary bias of the judge, shifts Lynn's position within the drama from villain to victim. In the final film, his advocacy of Bobby Mark makes his resistance heroic, while the clear agenda of the film – written in the context of the Hull prison riot – indicts the prison officers. It is impossible to watch the degradation of Lynn in this film without feeling sorrow and pity, and indeed, it is this film which audiences sampled by the BBC found most powerful. But there is something a little too inexorable about its unfolding.

While the series may not, quite, be 'sentimental about crooks', the last two films, the prison one in particular, are perhaps a little too directive. Just as Jack Lynn is confined to his cell, so too is the audience trapped into only one way of making sense of things. Despite the inventiveness of the film-making, as shown in the analysis of the 'slopping-out' scene, the dynamic between script and camera, the one insisting, the other 'not insisting' is less productive in this last film, as the location itself is so insistent, and the prison staff so uniformly unsympathetic. It is as if Jack can't get out, the camera can't stand back, and somehow, our understanding of the situation is confined to exactly what we are being shown. This criticism though, cannot be sustained over the final scene of the film, when Jack is shown working outside to plant a tree. The assignment of this relatively pleasant task indicates that Lynn is now compliant, and the film finishes with the newly planted copper beech tree in centre frame. Lynn looks back as he leaves, having been told that 'in ten, fifteen years, be a lovely tree

Jack Lynn looking back at the tree which will be lovely in 'ten, fifteen years'

there'. It is left for the viewer to work out that Lynn will still be there to see it.

Together, these films aim to produce an institutional analysis of the British criminal justice system in the 1970s. The generic forms through which institutions such as the police, the courts and prisons are normally shown on our screens are invoked and transformed to demonstrate the complex ecologies of custom and practice within which individuals act. The audience is led through a story about a professional armed robber as he comes to the attention of a detective and then the courts and prisons. The form of the films demonstrates the different levels of mediation between these professional worlds, while there is a consistent engagement with the question of the nature of evidence and its relation to power which must necessarily involve the viewer. *Law and Order* is like a backstory and a sequel ghosting the 'squealing tyres' of *The Sweeney*, and then moving on through the other institutions of criminal justice. How ironic then, that the way in which it is often remembered on television is as if it was *The Sweeney*. This is done through the repeated screening, in programmes about the police on British television, of one clip which edits together two parts of the first episode. The very opening – Inspector Pyall waiting at St James's Park tube station, is edited into the Terry Clark 'balls grab'. This clip is first shown in Bill Eagle's film about the British television police series, *Barlow, Regan, Pyall and Fancy* (BBC, tx 31/5/93). The same clip is then featured in *Call the Cops* (BBC, d. Kevin McMunigal, tx 12/8/08) and again in *How TV Changed Britain* (Silver River for Channel Four, d. G. J. Hughes, tx 1/6/08). It is this little montage which is used in these compilation programmes to introduce viewers to Inspector Pyall as the epitome of the corrupt detective, and suggest, misleadingly, that his principal mode of operation is through physical threat. As we have seen it is Pyall's brokering of information which is central, as he has the autonomy to judge which modes of criminality are more valuable 'licensed', and what a licence costs, whether cash or information. However, endless meetings are much less visually striking, and require much more screen time than a short clip affords, hence the elision of twelve minutes. Similarly, the striking ambition of *Law and Order* was to tell an institutional, rather than an individual, story, even though it was told through individuals. The way the clip is edited and used subsequently tends to shave the institutional from the individual. This representation of the series *Law and Order* reduces the programmes to what is telegenic in the contemporary television environment. It reminds us of the changing environment of television as a medium, which must make its material fit its formats, and, increasingly, deliver its material in as eye-catching and explicit manner as possible. The missing minutes bear mute witness to the privileged conditions under which *Law and Order* was made.

4 Reaction: Institutions of Criminal Justice and Institutions of Broadcasting

Tony Garnett's series "Law and Order" in which cops were indistinguishable from robbers and all lawyers bent and prison officers bullies, offended millions as was its intention. We can at least be grateful that the argot was so thick and the articulation so bad that much of the drama was incomprehensible. This tilt against authority has embarrassed the Governors of the BBC who confess their impotency.

Julian Critchley, MP, 'BBC at Battle Stations', *Daily Telegraph*, 19 June 1978

[W]ith a bit of luck the series will win enough international awards to protect its place in the archives.

Chris Dunkley, 'A Detective's Tale', *Financial Times*, 8 April 1978

While the makers of *Law and Order* might not concur with Julian Critchley's contention that it was their aim to offend millions, they did, evidently, want to 'tilt against authority', if that was required to get audiences thinking about the criminal justice system. While the films were in production, Garnett took advantage of his relatively autonomous position within the BBC to undertake the work discreetly. The system at the BBC in this period meant that it was the producer's responsibility to 'refer upwards' if it was thought there might be problems. Garnett observes drily, 'I didn't burden them', while Blair describes the way they were working as 'shooting on the quiet'.[67] In the latter stages of the production, with the decision not to broadcast *Scum* still reverberating, it is evident that there were rumours circulating about *Law and Order*. This can be seen from the writer Alan Plater's question to the BBC General Advisory Council on 8 February 1978, which was addressed to 'the BBC's Bureau of Missing Programmes', in which he referred to a 'film by Les Blair ... understood to be a piece concerned with prison life'.[68] The answer to Plater confirms that transmission is likely to take place, but also indicates that the BBC at this stage expected to frame the programmes as historical:

> [the series] is currently placed for transmission in week 14. The programmes are fictional but based on a plausible interpretation. I gather that, owing to the time that it takes to make programmes, combined with the rigorous action taken by Sir Robert Mark, it is accepted that the films may depict police behaviour of two years ago, rather than of today. The series is likely to be prefaced with some statement to this effect both on the screen and in the RT promotion.[69]

Evidently, 'two years ago' was, in the event ('are we saying it was real in 1975?'),[70] considered likely to provoke more questions than it would answer, and *Law and Order* was broadcast with no such preface. However this answer does indicate that the BBC was expecting some controversy, while at the same time accustomed to fielding strong responses to its productions. This final chapter will trace the way in which a television drama series about the institutions of criminal justice becomes caught up in the institutional autonomy of the BBC.

The BBC Duty Officer's log for 6 April, transmission night for 'A Detective's Tale', reports six phone calls, two of which were complimentary. Three callers complained about the programme, and the complaints are summarised as [the programme being] 'far too strong'. Three statements issued by police spokesmen (James Jardine from the Police Federation, Sir David McNee from Scotland Yard and the MP

Eldon Griffiths) immediately after this broadcast were widely quoted by newspapers the next day.[71] These responses belong to what can most usefully be considered the first phase of the *Law and Order* affair when, within the BBC, the complaints of predictable interested parties are seen as less significant than what the Director General refers to as 'the dogs that didn't bark'.[72] It is only after the final, prison episode that the tone begins to change with the transition marked by newspaper editorials about the state of British prisons in *The Observer* (30 April 1978) and *The Scotsman* (28 April 1978), and the Home Secretary Merlyn Rees, as the *Daily Mirror* reports it, launching 'a bitter attack on a TV crime series'.[73] The institutional response to the series thus took longer to build than accounts of spontaneous uproar suggest, and shows clear evidence of the mobilisation of professional bodies, notably the Police Federation, the Magistrates' Association and the Prison Officers' Association (POA).[74] The second phase is the afterlife of the programme from May 1978 to March 1980. In this period, the issue for the programme-makers is whether, as would be normal, it would be repeated within the two years for which original rights had been negotiated, and whether it would be made available for export and festival exhibition abroad. However for the BBC, the series becomes caught up in questions of, on the one hand, licence-fee renewal, and on the other, its ability to report on what is happening in prisons and its relations with the police.

Outside the press and television coverage, there is little trace of popular responses at the time, apart from the BBC's audience report in June 1978, and the memories of those who watched it. The distinguished criminologist Dick Hobbs told me that the series had been regarded as 'bang on' and 'like a documentary' by CID officers with whom he had been conducting fieldwork at the time.[75] The BBC calculated that the audience rose from 5.3 per cent to 8.5 per cent of the population (audiences between 2.5–3 million) and its audience report is very positive, suggesting that

> the increased panel audience for the last play especially would seem to have resulted from viewers' hearing or reading about the series and

> deciding to watch. Indeed several reporting on the final programme said how sorry they were to have missed one or more of the series and hoped it would be repeated.[76]

While the press reviews and features on the programmes are easily available, there are other, often determining responses, which are more difficult to find. The BBC has kept some records about the programme. There is nothing available about its production, but there is correspondence with interested parties during and after transmission, and references to the programme in the minutes of committees such as the Board of Management and the Board of Governors.[77] There are also recurrent references to *Law and Order* in the minutes of the News and Current Affairs Group which reveal that not only was the series an issue for external bodies and audiences, it was also controversial within the BBC. This I will discuss in more detail below, but must first note that in the relevant BBC files, key documents are missing. So there are little flurries of correspondence, often in the form of memos and annotated minutes, from which an inaugurating letter is missing. Several files commence with notes which state, 'Papers of a confidential nature have been removed from this file.' This means that it is difficult to assess how much direct pressure was being exerted on the BBC by the Home Office or what we could perhaps still call the establishment (borrowing from Critchley's invocation of 'authority') and what this pressure was focused on.

In the first phase, the BBC hierarchy is relatively sanguine. With Tony Garnett as producer, it is clear that it understood what the commission was likely to entail, as a memo the day after the first episode was transmitted from Brian Wenham, the Controller of BBC2 to Ian Trethowan, the Director General, suggests:

> The last part is in prison, and is said to have a little discreet violence. That episode may require a cut or two on grounds of violence, although I should stress that – Garnet [*sic*] being a clever lad – the violence will be skilfully underplayed.[78]

While the characterisation of the forty-two-year-old, non-Oxbridge Garnett as 'a clever lad' is eloquent in terms of the class culture of the BBC, recognition of his authorship recurs in the internal discussion, when, for example, Trethowan describes the series as being 'made in Tony Garnett's customary pseudo-realistic style'.[79] It is the 'pseudo-realistic style' which is of great concern to institutional complainants, usually on behalf of other more naive viewers, and this is also the focus of the BBC's special *Arena* discussed in Chapter 1. The BBC's own audience research (available in June 1978) however, does not indicate that the audience had difficulty in understanding the stylistic propositions of the series. Indeed the researchers observe that

> [w]hatever their feelings about the way in which the police were portrayed, those reporting were clearly impressed by the quality of the writing and the 'superb, understated' acting and production, many warmly welcoming this first play as vastly superior to the usual 'sugary' fictional crime series, both British and American.[80]

The 'reaction index', which is the way in which the BBC assesses audience approbation, rises from sixty-three for the first film to eighty-three for the last.[81] The researchers were evidently briefed to enquire into stylistic issues, and observe the following:

> Certainly, judging from viewers' comments, the very realistic 'documentary' style of these plays, together with the universally commended portrayal of the characters by actors largely unknown to those reporting, may have made the themes of corruption and abuse of power more readily believable than an obviously fictional treatment.[82]

Internally, the BBC compares the realism of the early episodes with other recent plays. In comparison with the untransmitted *Scum*, it is declared favourably that 'this could have been a slice of a real detective's week, whereas *Scum* had no credibility at all', although at this same meeting, some anxiety is expressed about the portrayal of A10 in the programme.[83] The following week, Jim Allen's play *The Spongers* (also produced by Garnett) is mentioned, when it is noted in contrast that '*Law and Order* has no really good characters' and the Director General reports that the 'Board [of Governors] had been notably unfussed about the programme'.[84] Indeed, in the subsequent meeting of the Governors, the Director General is minuted as being 'rather puzzled by the fact that there had been so few complaints'.[85]

After the BBC has arranged a screening at Westminster for MPs such as Eldon Griffiths to watch 'what appears to have been a programme showing the police as a complete bunch of crooks',[86] Griffiths writes a long, thoughtful letter, querying the public-service aspects of the broadcast but conceding, 'Every single item you showed in the "Detective's Tale" was probably true – save the highly improper (and in my view exceedingly foolish) insinuations against the A10 Division.'[87] So the complaint against the series, in its initial phase, from the Parliamentary Representative of the Police Federation, is not that none of it is true – far from it – but that crucially, the series suggests that even the internal police investigatory body, only established in 1972 by the reforming outsider, Sir Robert Mark, is corrupt.

This initial period of courteous complaints, statements by police representatives and fairly predictable newspaper reaction comes to an end after an interview with Newman on Radio London (which does not survive) of which the Director General scribbles on another letter from Griffiths 'this makes us a bit vulnerable I fear' (20 April 1978), the screening of the final, prison episode and the questions in parliament. This mention of 'vulnerability' is the first hint of the strategic decisions that will follow.

The debate in the House of Lords, initiated by Patrick Gordon Walker, is about whether the government should 'make representations to the BBC about the recent *Law and Order* series on BBC Television, and in particular about the attacks made therein on the reputation of the Police and Prison Service',[88] and Lord Harris, for the Home Office, invokes the 'long-established principle that responsibility for the content of programmes is a matter for the broadcasting authorities', while also declaring, of the complaints by the police and prison service, that 'I shall make quite sure that the BBC is left in no doubt on this particular matter.'[89] Of the responsibilities of the Home Office, Harris privileges the police and prison service over the BBC:

> I would certainly not imagine for a moment that there was even the remotest relationship between what one saw on television and the magnificent job which the British Police Service does for all the people of this country. Indeed the same remarks apply so far as the Prison Service is concerned.[90]

He also reports the view of the Home Secretary that 'the content of some of the elements of these programmes were [sic], to put it at its very least, unhelpful'.[91] 'Unhelpful' is an interesting choice of word for a sentence which omits – and assumes – a predicate which is presumably something like 'the maintenance of law and order'. These are high stakes, and evidently recur in communications with the BBC about the programmes, for three days later on 11 May 1978 the Director General drafts a letter to Eldon Griffiths which includes the following:

> I was very grateful to you for sending me, with your letter of 3rd May, a copy of your note to the Home Secretary about the possible threats to public order which might arise during a General Election [*note not available*]. We are frankly very concerned about this danger here, and deeply conscious of our own position.

This paragraph finally appears in a letter sent to Griffiths on 18 May, in answer to a third letter from Griffiths in which his tone has changed completely. Far from the reflective tone of the first letter, in which he offers 'to discuss these difficult matters if you think it would help' (18 April 1978), the judgment is now much harsher: 'No single emission by the media has done so much to damage public confidence in the Police (or for that matter, the BBC) for a very long time.'[92] He goes on to demand an apology, observing that '[r]esponsibility demands that somehow, the Corporation should set the record straight, and make amends to those whom the series so viciously traduced'.

It seems that the decision neither to repeat the series, nor to export it, was partly the result of external pressure and partly the result of the BBC's own judgment about its vulnerability in this period. The MP Julian Critchley, a constant critic of the BBC, was active on more than one front, writing newspaper articles and letters to the BBC. Some of these are not available for scrutiny, but something of their tenor and effect can be deduced from notes such as an undated handwritten memo from Chairman Michael Swann to the Director General, referring to a letter of 26 June 1978 which is not in the files.

> Please see attached letter from Julian Critchley. I would have thought that selling 'Law and Order' all over the place was most unwise, and putting it into an exhibition fairly unwise. The Iron Curtain countries would love every minute of it. Should you wield the heavy hand?[93]

Thus in addition to questions about social stability in Britain, opponents of the series have also raised questions about its portrayal of a Western democracy for the Eastern bloc countries.

To some extent, the BBC internal discussions and responses to criticism about the plays have a practised air – this is not the first fuss caused by the output of the Drama Group, nor will it be the last. Replies sent by senior BBC figures, such as the Director General and the Deputy Managing Director Television (Alastair Milne) to letters from prison governors, the Magistrates' Association and the Police Federation, or points made to the Board of Governors, the Board of Management and the General Advisory Council usually concede that the plays were insufficiently identified as fiction in their initial presentation, and then proceed to make three points: an argument about the overall balance of BBC output; an insistence that the view taken by the plays is 'subjective', and that they are the work of an acclaimed and recognised artist (Garnett); and the citing of particular programmes, particularly *Porridge*, as counterweights.[94]

One of the ways in which the BBC can justify the licence fee is through sustaining a complex ecology which supports both 'balanced' reporting of news and current affairs and often strongly voiced dramatic output. These forms of programming have historically been produced by different departments within the BBC, each with their own professional culture. The institutional tension, which is particularly evident in Garnett's work, is that a dynamic, contemporary television story-telling, which aspires to convince its viewers of its truth, inevitably engages with the look of news-and-current-affairs television.[95] Whilst it might have been more convenient for those who wanted to maintain a clear binary opposition between documentary/truth and drama/fiction if television drama had stayed in the studio and had not used film, the excitement and achievement of this television drama presses precisely at these boundaries. The issue about *Law and Order*, which Milne refers to in the *Arena* special, 'When Is a Play Not a Play' as 'a matter of labelling', is seen to be the way in which the style of the films disrupts these distinctions, and much of the BBC's defence adopts the strategy of accepting fault over 'labelling' while defending this 'subjective' vision. However, this familiar BBC path in defence of television drama is disrupted by the reaction of the Prison Officers' Association to the final film. This film, with its 'repeatedly sombre representation of Prison Officers', to quote from Richard Clutterbuck, a member of the BBC's General Advisory Council and a committed political opponent of 'Tony Garnett and his friends',[96] causes considerable protest, and the POA resolves, at its annual conference in May, to block BBC access to its premises until the end of the year. While this resolution has few consequences for the Drama Group – indeed, we have already noted how 'unhelpful' the Home Office was in the matter of prison filming – it has immediate repercussions for the News and Current Affairs Group. The first instance takes the form of the disruption of a long-running *Inside Story* project about the parole board which was just moving into its final stages. In this project, the producer Rex Bloomstein had been following four prisoners at Wormwood Scrubs, with Home Office approval, as they moved towards the possibility of parole. According to

Peter Fiddick, the first the BBC learns of the ban is when Bloomstein arrives to film one of the prisoner's parole board appearances on 22 May and is refused entry.[97] However, following rioting at HMP Gartree (a maximum-security prison) in October, the full implications of the ban become clearer. On this occasion, BBC reporters and cameras were not permitted into the prison, or to the briefings offered to the rest of the press, and this exclusion becomes a repeated topic of discussion at meetings of News and Current Affairs (10, 17, 24 and 31 October, 28 November and 19 December 1978). The minutes don't reveal the terms of discussion after the brief, but a revealing minute appears in the meeting of 6 June, when a comment regretting that the 'increasing tendency of the public to confuse factual and fictional programmes' is followed by the sharp observation that in this instance 'the Drama Department has itself confused fiction with fact'.[98] This distinction is one which, to the evident frustration of the BBC, the POA also refuses to make, with Michael Bunce (the Head of Information Services, Television) reporting to News and Current Affairs, on 10 October 1978, immediately after the BBC's humiliating exclusion from Gartree, that 'the POA has refused to distinguish between factual and fictional programmes'.[99]

Adding to difficulties with the prison officers come demands from the police that it should have what amounts to script approval. Again, it is the News and Current Affairs Group that is most immediately affected, with *Law and Order* mentioned by name, in a long meeting in July 1978 with the Deputy Assistant Commissioner, Peter Nievens[100] to discuss a proposed new contract. This is then followed by a meeting at Scotland Yard for the Director General, of which it is reported, 'what the police now wanted was the opportunity to see programmes before transmission and to comment on them'.[101] The detail of these discussions, which finally become public in June 1979 initially through the radical magazine *The Leveller* cannot further detain us nor is it possible to know from available records how the BBC's agreement to consultation and previewing, while retaining editorial control, was put into practice. The point is that this is an instance in which the distinction between fact and fiction occupies a range of differently placed institutional voices, and in which a dramatic series produces repercussions which, for the BBC, are most serious in relation to its capacity to fulfil its brief in relation to news reporting. The question of the repeats and possible overseas sales of the programme becomes the symbolic currency through which the BBC is seen to express public contrition, as shown, for example, in a *Sunday Telegraph* report in June 1979 (i.e. more than a year after transmission), headlined, 'BBC Bans Export of Crime Series'.[102]

Within the BBC, support for a repeat is bolstered by research about 'A Detective's Tale' which 'has indicated that the plays in fact left public respect for the Police undiminished',[103] and this is presented in a *Television World* broadcast in June 1979 with commentary from guests including Sir Robert Mark, Richard Hoggart and Alastair Milne. Milne's public refusal to commit to a repeat is reported as 'no repeat' (for example by the *Sunday Telegraph*), but in fact, from July 1979 the question of a repeat for the series, with or without sale abroad, is being discussed by the BBC across a range of committees, with Milne in favour, suggesting scheduling it against *Match of the Day*.[104] This progresses to a confidential formal paper tabled by Robin Scott to the Board of Management in November 1979 which proposes to repeat 'the distinguished fictional drama series *Law and Order*' – quietly, late on Sunday nights in February – with a request that the Board take a view before the proposal goes forward to the Governors. The BBC hierarchy clearly felt that it must have the informed support of both the Board of Management and the Governors before proceeding, and it is also proposed that the programmes can now be offered for sale overseas, 'on the strict understanding that some explanation that the works are fiction will also be broadcast'. The Board of Management decides to support 'scheduling a repeat at a politically sensible time. The BBC would not publicise its intentions to repeat in the present danger period.' Even this cautious decision, with its explicit reference to 'the present danger period' (presumably that of awaiting the licence fee and the Broadcasting Bill), was then challenged by Michael Swann on behalf of

News and Current Affairs, with a scribbled note, 'Peter Marshall (Home Office) and Rex Bloomstein are about to agree a "fly on the wall" about prison service. If the L&O series is repeated, POA will withdraw.'[105]

However, the increased vulnerability of the BBC's position 'in the present danger period' is made clear when the confidential Board of Management minutes of 12 November 1979 record: 'Acting Director General said that the Board of Governors, with a few dissentients, and with some reluctance, had concluded that a series that could be repeated could not be withheld from sale abroad.' There were, in November 1979, continuing strategic reasons for the BBC to avoid antagonising the May-elected Conservative government. One of the first actions of this government had been to grant in full a pay rise to the police, thereby indicating its priorities. The BBC had applied for a licence fee rise to £40–41 (colour) (from £25) and £2 on black and white, following the disappointing settlement in 1978 from Merlyn Rees; and the government White Paper on the future of broadcasting (which was published in February 1980) was in the final draft stages. As the Board of Management meeting quoted above continues,

> But the Chairman, mindful of the current political climate, had instructed him [Acting DG] to take no action on the Board's decision before the next regular Board Meeting. The Deputy Managing Director of Television made it clear that no action would have been taken in any case before the licence fee settlement was announced.[106]

The new licence fee of £34 for two years is announced on 23 November, and the BBC Director of Finance has a 'bleak' meeting with the Home Office.[107] Privately, the new Conservative Home Secretary, Willie Whitelaw, is thanked for his prompt announcement of a two-year settlement,[108] and BBC staff are informed that there should be 'no bleating' about the amount.[109] No researchers are permitted access to any files after 1979 at the BBC Written Archives Centre. The White Paper which leads to the creation of Channel 4 is published in early February 1980, and later that month, the BBC announces 9 per cent cuts across the board – £130,000,000.[110] *Law and Order* is finally repeated, very quietly, late on Sunday nights, in March 1980, just before the rights expire. *The Radio Times* billing for the 1980 repeat includes the prominent labelling: 'Playhouse Presents', and the description of the series has, interestingly, changed from being 'Four *films* about the law' to 'Four *plays* about the law' (my italics).[111] Clearly, plays are thought to be more fictional than films. In my view this Sunday night repeat in March 1980, three months after an inadequate, if not unexpected, licence fee settlement and the publication of the Broadcasting Bill, is eloquent. Either 'the present danger' period was judged to be over with the announcement of funding and remit for the BBC – or perhaps, which would be a more accurate view of the position of the BBC in the 1980s, there was no end in sight, and so the BBC might as well publish and be damned.[112]

So *Law and Order* was repeated after all. It is however, not just for the BBC in the period 1978–80 that the 'no repeat/no export' line is significant. It is very prevalent in commentary that is sympathetic to *Law and Order*, and I think this is because it makes the programmes seem 'harder'. As I have found myself, it is much easier to write or say, 'never been seen since' than to have to add, 'huge fuss but then there was a surprise late-night repeat two years later for very complicated reasons'. But the other attractions of 'banned'? It is simpler and more declarative, and testifies to the series' impact. Like Jack Lynn's idea of doing prison, that's doing television the hard way.

There are some concluding points to make about the controversy ignited by *Law and Order* in 1978. Given the enormous care taken by the production team 'to make something many perceived as shocking literally matter of fact', as Les Blair put it,[113] the first point is that it worked: they managed to both shock and convince. While much attention at the time was concentrated on the excellence of writing, direction and performance in achieving this effect (even if it was simultaneously deplored for the better misleading audiences), it is also important to consider the overall structure of the series. For what *Law and Order* does is to weave together, as one coherent story, the many glimpses of trouble in the criminal justice system which would have been available to any contemporary newspaper reader or television-news viewer. The Scotland Yard scandals, the widely publicised campaigns against the conviction of George Davis – whose supporters at one point dug up the hallowed turf of a Test Match ground, the prison treatment of George Ince, prison riots at Hull and Gartree: all of these stories were already in the public domain, testimony of trouble, reported as disconnected flashes of criminal behaviour, protest and violence. *Law and Order* dared to imagine putting them all together in the fictional story of Jack Lynn as evidence of widespread, systemic institutional corruption. The four weeks of the broadcasts, with the complex intertwining of deals, although focused through the fate of one man, have, as their ambition, an analysis of how institutions work, so that all those little glimpses of trouble with criminal justice begin to seem part of a whole. Television long-form drama can provide the space for this institutional analysis, building, week by week, for an audience who must, in real time, wait to find out what happens next, and this is an example of a mode of television story-telling which is formed within the public service imperatives to inform, educate and entertain.

The second point, which Tony Garnett makes on *Criminal Minds*, is that in relation to the Metropolitan Police in the 1970s, the film-makers were substantially vindicated. The un-*Dixon* like world of policing depicted in *Law and Order* had surfaced in a series of scandals about the detective culture of the Met in which the entrepreneurial autonomy of a 'firm within a firm', the payment to policemen for licences (particularly in Soho), the systematic use of informants and various forms of 'turn-taking' in relation to prosecutions had been revealed.[114] It was this culture, within the CID, that Robert Mark had set out to destroy, and to which later legislation, such as the 1984 Police and Criminal Evidence Act (PACE), (which, for example, makes it a requirement to tape interviews with suspects), was addressed. The police corruption trials of the 1970s were followed, after Mark's retirement, by the establishment of yet another inquiry into police corruption, Operation Countryman, in the summer of 1978. The notably inconclusive results of Countryman, with only two convictions, were accompanied by a series of allegations that the inquiry had met internal obstruction.[115] Countryman, however, was cited by more than one newspaper journalist as the reason why *Law and Order* was unexpectedly repeated in March 1980. Indeed Frank Williamson, the ex-Chief Constable of Cumbria, who had been appointed to head one of the previous inquiries into the Met (a story dramatised by Peter Flannery in *Our Friends in the North*, BBC, 1996) is quoted in the short-lived newspaper *Now* as saying that he would not be watching the repeat because it was too accurate.[116]

The debates I have traced reveal something about the complexity of power, and the ways in which an institution such as the BBC in this period is internally differentiated, with different strata and sections aligning themselves with, and answerable to, a range of internal and external bodies and power blocs in a period of considerable uncertainty. It is difficult to recover now the volatility of the context of Britain in the late 1970s; but then, no-one knew that what would happen next, with the 1979 election, would be what is now called Thatcherism. When I read the BBC files about the decision not to screen *Scum*, I felt, to my surprise, a rush of memory about leftist attitudes to the BBC in the 1970s, as what I was reading, in these (censored) files seemed to be the deliberations of a ruling elite in which there was common cause between the hierarchy of the BBC and the Home Office, the two united against the broadcast of this thoroughly researched play about the brutality of the borstal system. As David Hare observed,

> the decision about *Scum* was particularly craven, it was a pure political decision dressed up as an artistic decision … . And once you had the simple equation – the Home Office licenses the BBC, therefore you cannot make films which are critical of Home Office institutions – then the BBC's credibility was destroyed.[117]

The *Law and Order* files don't read like this. Instead, internal BBC discussion moves from a relatively sanguine tone to that of an institution increasingly under siege. The prison officers' action disrupts news reporting, humiliates the Corporation, and brings to a fresh head a long-running conflict between two departments about the ethics, and ownership, of documentary form. The continuing anxiety in the Corporation about the consequences of the Annan Report and the licence-fee settlement takes on new intensity with the May election of the 1979 Conservative government. What starts off as a story about four films made about the institutions of criminal justice slowly transforms into a story about another institution, the BBC, and the fragility of its independence from government. The *Law and Order* files read as if the BBC doesn't want – 'with reluctance' – to further antagonise the government once the police and the prison officers are involved.

The final point to make about the response to the series is that it represents an exemplary instance of broadcast television fiction as a national event. The sound and fury of the reaction demonstrates why writers, directors, producers and other creative personnel wanted to work in television in this period, on what Garnett identified as 'a platform as big and as politically important as this one'.[118] Because of public service –rather than market – imperatives within the organisation of the BBC, however fraught and difficult some of the passages between production and repeat were, the makers had been able to work in relative freedom to create films which told shocking stories about the central institutions of criminal justice in the country. Week by week, audiences had watched programmes that were, ultimately, about government and power. Millions of people watched the films, and millions more heard about them. The debate about the typicality of what was shown involved popular arguments about aesthetics, politics, policing, the law and the penal system. And of course, about styles and forms of television. This surely is an instance of classic television produced by British public service broadcasting.

Notes

1 *Criminal Minds: The Making of Law and Order*, prod. Steve Broster, 2008, 2Entertain, included on *G. F. Newman's Law and Order* BBC DVD, BBC Worldwide Ltd, distributed under licence by 2Entertain, 2008 (henceforth *Criminal Minds*).

2 Patrick Gordon Walker, '"Law and Order": Police and Prison Services', *Hansard* (House of Lords Official Report) vol. 391 no. 74 (8 May 1978): col. 671.

3 G. F. Newman jokes about the format fee he is owed by Dick Wolf (the producer of the US *Law & Order*) in *Mark Lawson Talks to G. F. Newman* (11 August 2008). Newman's website states 'LAW AND ORDER subsequently spawned the huge hit American version making it the most successful television brand ever' (<www.gfnewman.com>, accessed 10 October 2009).

4 'This Week', *Radio Times* vol. 219 no. 2838 (1–7 April 1978): 3.

5 My account draws, in particular, on Andy Beckett, *When the Lights Went Out* (London: Faber, 2009); Ross McKibbin (various), including 'Homage to Wilson and Callaghan', *London Review of Books* vol. 13 no. 20 (October 1991): 3–5; James Thomas, '"Bound by History": The Winter of Discontent in British Politics, 1979–2004', *Media Culture and Society* vol. 29 no. 2 (2007): 263–83; Jim Tomlinson, *The Politics of Decline: Understanding Post-war Britain* (Harlow: Longman, 2000).

6 For example, at the British Academy discussion evening, 'Reassessing the 1970s', London, 23 September 2009.

7 There are inconsistencies in the spelling of Pyall's name. I will follow the film credits and the *Radio Times*, although in the novelised version of *Law and Order* (by Newman), the name is spelled 'Pyle'.

8 *Radio Times* vol. 219 no. 2838 (1–7 April 1978): 53.

9 Shaun Sutton discusses what he calls 'all film plays', *The Largest Theatre in the World: Thirty Years of Television Drama* (London: BBC, 1982), p. 89.

10 G. F. Newman, 'If the Face Fits', *Radio Times* vol. 219 no. 2838 (1–7 April 1978): 5.

11 BBC WAC R78/2,072/1, letter from Eldon Griffiths asking for screening in the Westminster cinema, 11/4/1978.

12 Dave Rolinson gives an account of the vicissitudes of *Scum* in his book *Alan Clarke* (Manchester: Manchester University Press, 2005), pp. 74–87.

13 WAC T41/511/1 *Scum*, 1977–8: 'I admire your nerve but not your judgement', A. Milne to M. Matheson, 10 February 1978; Madeleine Macmurragh-Kavanagh '"Drama into News": Strategies of Intervention in *The Wednesday Play*', *Screen* vol. 38 no. 3 (1997): 247–59.

14 WAC R2/31/3, BBC Board of Management Minutes, 11 September 1978, item 614: 'DG said that the PM's decision not to have a General Election in October has changed the nature of the BBC's licence fee strategy.'

15 On Annan, see Des Freedman, *Television Policies of the Labour Party 1951–2001* (London: Frank Cass, 2003), pp. 97–115 and Lord Annan *Report of the Committee on the Future* *of Broadcasting* Cmnd 6753 (London: HMSO, 1977).

16 'BBC Reveals Its Anxiety over the Next Licence Fee', leader, *Television Today*, 25 May 1978: 19.

17 Robert Reiner, *The Politics of the Police*, 3rd edn (Oxford: Oxford University Press, 2000), p. 157; in contrast, it is not mentioned in either John Caughie's *Television Drama: Realism, Modernism, and British Culture* (Oxford: Oxford University Press, 2000) or Mulvey and Sexton's *Experimental Television* (Manchester: Manchester University Press, 2007).

18 Lez Cooke, *British Television Drama: A History* (London: BFI, 2003) provides the first discussion, grouping it with two Euston Films productions, *Out* (Thames, 1978) and *The Sweeney* (1975–8), pp. 113–18.

19 *The Times*, 20 January 1950: 8, cited by Clive Emsley, *The English Police: A Political and Social History* (Harlow: Longman, 1996), p. 170; Sir Robert Mark, *In the Office of Constable* (London: Collins, 1978), p. 52.

20 John McGrath, quoted in Cooke, *British Television Drama*, p. 57.

21 *Criminal Minds*.

22 Dick Hobbs, 'Stealing Commercial Cash: From Safecracking to Armed Robbery', in F. Brookman *et al.* (eds), *Handbook on Crime* (Cullompton: Willan, 2010).

23 Hugo Young, *One of Us* (London: Macmillan, 1991), p. 238.

24 My sources in this section are: Cox *et al.*, *The Fall of Scotland Yard* (Harmondsworth: Penguin, 1977); Emsley, *The English Police*; Dick Hobbs, *Doing the Business: Entrepreneurship, the Working Class and Detectives in the East End of London* (Oxford: Oxford University Press, 1988); Mark, *In the Office of Constable*; Philip Rawlings, *Policing: A Short History* (Cullompton: Willan, 2002) and *Crime and Power: A History of Criminal Justice 1688–1998* (Harlow: Longman, 1999); Reiner, *The Politics of the Police*.

25 Garry Lloyd and Julian Mounter, 'Tapes Reveal Planted Evidence', *The Times*, 29 November 1969: 1; 'Bribes, Threats, Planted Gelignite': *The Times*, 29 November 1969: 6.

26 Lloyd and Mounter, 'Bribes, Threats, Planted Gelignite': 6.

27 Mark, *In the Office of Constable*, pp. 144–62.

28 Staff reporter, 'Doctor Says Ince Case Is Terrifying', *The Times*, 19 August 1977: 4; No author, 'Home Office Denies Drugs Were Forced on Mr Ince', *The Times*, 20 August 1977: 3.

29 See, for example, *Panorama*: 'The Crisis Inside', tx 28/2/1977 (reporter Ludovic Kennedy).

30 Les Blair to author, 26 November 2008. Unreferenced quotations in this chapter from Blair or Garnett are taken from meetings on 25 and 26 November 2008.

31 *Barlow, Regan, Pyall and Fancy* (produced and directed by Bill Eagles, 31 May 1993).

32 G. F. Newman to author, 13 November 2009.

33 Mike Leigh, contribution to obituary, Simon Channing Williams, *The Guardian*, 15 April 2009: 34.

34 John Hill, 'Interview with Ken Loach', in George McKnight (ed.), *Agent of Challenge and Defiance* (Trowbridge: Flicks Books, 1997), p. 161.

35 Les Blair, from Paul Madden's NFT 1976 'Programme Notes for a Season of British Television Drama 1959–1973', cited by S. Lacey, *Tony Garnett* (Manchester: Manchester University Press, 2007), p. 97.

36 Vincent Porter,'The Context of Creativity: Ealing Studios and Hammer Films', in James Curran and Vincent Porter (eds), *British Cinema History* (London: Weidenfeld and Nicolson, 1983), p. 180.
37 Sydney Newman memo to Michael Peacock, 31 March 1966, BBC WAC T5/695/2, cited by Macmurraugh Kavanagh, '"Drama" into "News"': 249.
38 Caughie, *Television Drama*, p. 135.
39 Tony Garnett in *Call the Cops* episode one (BBC, d. Kevin McMunigal, 2008).
40 Tony Garnett in *Barlow, Regan, Pyall and Fancy* (1993).
41 Interview with author, 25 November 2008.
42 Lacey, *Tony Garnett*, p. 2.
43 See Stuart Laing, 'Ken Loach: Histories and Contexts' in McKnight, *Agent of Challenge and Defiance*, p. 17.
44 Trevor Griffiths, 'The Party', in *Plays One* (London: Faber and Faber, 1996), p. 166.

45 Kennedy Martin in 1978, cited by Lez Cooke, *Troy Kennedy Martin* (Manchester: Manchester University Press, 2007), p. 124; G. F. Newman's *The Guvnor* (London: Hart-Davis MacGibbon, 1977) acknowledges that parts had previously appeared as a screenplay co-written with Troy Kennedy Martin.
46 *Mark Lawson Talks to G. F. Newman.*
47 G. F. Newman in *Crime Writers* no. 5, 'Police Story' (BBC, tx 3/12/1978), producer Bernard Adams.
48 *Mark Lawson Talks to G. F. Newman.*
49 Blair's other early work included direction for Alan Bleasdale's *Early to Bed* (BBC, 1975) and Brian Glover's *Sunshine in Brixton* (Thames, 1976).
50 The Ken Campbell Road Show in the early 1970s was followed in 1976 by the eight-hour epic 'Illuminatus' (co-written with Chris Langham).
51 Tony Garnett to author, 25 November 2008.
52 Les Blair, email to author 28 November 2008.
53 Hazel Holt, 'The BBC a Prime Offender in the Area of Half-truths', *Stage and Television Today*, 27 April 1978, p. 13.
54 *Criminal Minds*, and telephone conversation with author, 15 October 2009. George Davis, a professional criminal, was released (but not declared innocent) in 1976 after a high-profile campaign. Similarities between Lynn and Davis were such that the BBC house journal, *Ariel*, headed an article on *Law and Order* 'Jack Lynn Is Not George Davis – OK?', 3 May 1978, quoting Les Blair. George Ince was convicted in 1972 for a bullion robbery on identification evidence and his prison treatment was also the subject of a campaign. Saunders acted for Ince.
55 Margaret Matheson, in Richard Kelly (ed.), *Alan Clarke* (London: Faber and Faber, 1998), p. 104. Mangold had made a series of films about prison, including a scrupulous *Panorama* programme on the 1976 Hull prison riot, 'What Happened at Hull' (tx 24/1/1977).
56 *Criminal Minds.*
57 An exception here is Laurie Taylor writing in *New Society* at the end of the series: 'Partners in Crime', 27 April 1978.
58 Ted Willis, speaking in *Crime Writers*: 'Police Story'. He observes that 'No police series has ever told the truth about the police; it can't do', and cites the 1956 *Dixon* 'Rotten Apple' as the permitted 'mild form' of what he wanted to do.
59 John Caughie, *Television Drama*, p. 122.
60 In the 1994 BBC series *The Underworld*, the first episode, 'Thieves' (tx 16/2/94) introduces the convicted criminal Frankie Fraser as a man who 'prides himself on

never having earned a day's remission in prison'. This take on prison is the one to which the old lag, Fletcher (Ronnie Barker), in *Porridge,* is contrasted.

61 Tony Garnett and Ken Campbell speaking in *Criminal Minds.*

62 Jason Jacobs, *Body Trauma TV: The New Hospital Dramas* (London: BFI, 2003), p. 42–3.

63 *Radio Times*, vol. 219 no. 2838 (1–7 April 1978): 3–4.

64 Les Blair to author, 26 November 2008.

65 Diana Geddes, 'George Ince Case May Be Re-examined, MP Says', *The Times*, 28 February 1977, p. 3.

66 Tony Garnett quoted by Victoria Radin in 'Briefs and Blaggers', *The Observer*, 2 April 1978.

67 Interviews with the author, Garnett, 25 November 2008, Blair, 26 November 2008.

68 WAC T41/511/1, Memo from D. B. Mann to M.D.Tel., 31 January 1978. Other programmes Plater names included Dennis Potter's *Brimstone & Treacle* (1982) and Spike Milligan's *The Melting Pot* (1975).

69 WAC T41/511/1 note from Roger Cary for the M.D.Tel. to reply to Plater, 3 February 1978.

70 WAC R78/2,072/1, memo from Brian Wenham to the DG, 7 April 1978.

71 For example, *Daily Express*, 8 April 1978, *Daily Telegraph*, 7 April 1978; *Evening News*, 7 April 1978; *Belfast Telegraph*, 7 April 1978; *Daily Mail*, 8 April 1978.

72 WAC R2/31/2 DG, Board of Management minutes, 8 May 1978, item 343.

73 Mirror Reporter, 'Outlaw and Order', *Daily Mirror*, 3 May 1978. Speech also reported in *The Times* and *Financial Times.* The BBC records twenty-seven complaints and nineteen 'appreciations' after 'A Prisoner's Tale' (TV Weekly Review Board, 3 May 1978).

74 Letters on file (in addition to the correspondence with Eldon Griffiths), include those from Leeds POA, 22 April 1978, the Governor of Manchester Prison, 16 May 1978, and the Magistrates' Association, 11 October 1978.

75 Meeting, 6 November 2008 with Dick Hobbs, author of *Doing the Business: Entrepreneurship, The Working Class and Detectives in the East End of London* (Oxford: Oxford University Press, 1988).

76 WAC R78/2,072/1, 'An Audience Research Report, Weeks 14–17, *Law and Order*' VR/78/220, 26 June 1978, p. 1. The viewing figures are given as percentages of a population of 50,500,000. ITV was attracting about 8 per cent in the same slot. The figure for 'A Detective's Tale' is similar to that for *M*A*S*H* (1972–83) shown on BBC2 at 10.25 pm on Saturday night in the same week.

77 These have been subsequently collated in a programme file, WAC R78/2,072/1; I have cross-checked with other files such as Board of Management (BOM) and News and Current Affairs (NCA) minutes, which is why some items are referenced to R78/2,072/1 and some to BOM minutes or NCA.

78 WAC R78/2,072/1, memo from Brian Wenham to the DG, 7 April 1978.

79 WAC R78/2,072/1DG, BOM minutes, 10 April 1978.

80 'An Audience Research Report', p. 2

81 'Reaction Indices' were based on questionnaires completed by a sample of the audience.

82 'An Audience Research Report', p. 3.

83 WAC R78/2,072/1, BOM minutes, 10 April 1978.

84 WAC R78/2,072/1DG, BOM minutes, 17 April 1978.

85 WAC R78/2,072/1 Board of Governors, meeting minutes, 11 May 1978.

86 WAC R78/2,072/1 Eldon Griffiths letter, 11 April 1978.
87 WAC R78/2,072/1, Eldon Griffiths to Roger Cary, 18 April 1978.
88 Gordon Walker, '"Law and Order"': column 671.
89 Newman said that Harris summoned the DG to the Home Office in *Mark Lawson Talks to G. F. Newman*.
90 *Hansard* vol. 391 no. 74 (8 May 1978): column 671.
91 Lord Harris, *Hansard* vol. 391 no. 74 (8 May 1978): column 671.
92 WAC R78/2,072/1 Eldon Griffiths to DG, 11 May 1978.
93 WAC R78/2,072/1 Michael Swann memo, undated, *c.* 26 June 1978.
94 *Porridge* (BBC1, 1974–7) created and written by Dick Clement and Ian La Frenais, was a popular prison-set situation comedy which starred Ronnie Barker as the 'old lag' Fletcher. It is mentioned in nearly every BBC answer to complaints about *Law and Order.*
95 Garnett and the News and Current Affairs Group had a long history of disagreement. Most germane is the '*Five Women/ Some Women*' affair in the late 1960s, which involved acted testimonies of recidivist women, and was declared to be 'not a play, nor is it a documentary', thus delaying transmission until it was cut (Garnett interview and WAC T51/113 Music and Arts, *Some Women*).
96 WAC R78/2,072/1: Richard Clutterbuck in General Advisory Council minutes, 26 April 1978.
97 Peter Fiddick, 'Police and Prison Officers Are up in Arms about How BBC Programmes like *Law and Order* Spoil Their Image: What They Want is Censorship', *The Guardian*, 24 July 1978. Fiddick was confidentially briefed about the POA in a letter from Michael Bunce (WAC R78/2, 072/1, 19 July 1978).
98 WAC: minutes, NCA, 6 June 1978.
99 WAC: minutes, NCA, 10 October 1978.
100 WAC: minutes, NCA, 11 July 1978, part II; 17 July 1978, item 526.
101 WAC: minutes, NCA, 1 August 1978, item 391.
102 'BBC Bans Export of Crime Series' 'By Our Television Staff', *Sunday Telegraph*, 24 June 1979.
103 There seems to be no trace of the research in the BBC Archives, but Tannenbaum outlines it at some length in *Television World*, tx 22/6/1979.
104 WAC R78/2,072/1, Alastair Milne to DG, 2 July 1979.
105 WAC R78/2,072/1,Michael Swann handwritten note re. BOM discussion, 5 November 1979, C23, 8 November 1979.
106 WAC R78/2,072/1, BOM minutes, 12 November 1979, item 774.
107 WAC R2/32/3, BOM minutes, 3 December 1979, p. 5.
108 WAC R78/1,125/1, Michael Swann to W. Whitelaw, 23 November 1979, D3 81-1.
109 WAC R78/1,125/1, BBC Press Office, 23 November 1979, note with BBC statement on licence fee.
110 'Zings Go Strings on BBC's Purse', *Broadcast*, 10 March 1980: 3. Leader (no author).
111 *Radio Times*, 9 March 1980: 37.
112 Chris Dunkley of the *Financial Times*, 12 March 1980, pointed out that the repeat of a 'A Detective's Tale' was preceded by the radical documentarist Philip Donnellan's *Gone for a Soldier* (1984), hypothesising that the BBC thinking was, 'if one is to be hanged, it might as well be for two sheep as a lamb'.
113 Les Blair, email to author, 28 November 2008.

114 Cox *et al.*, *The Fall of Scotland Yard* (Harmondsworth: Penguin, 1977); Reiner, *The Politics of the Police*, pp. 6–64.
115 Reiner argues that Countryman 'cast doubt on any idea that the endemic corruption in the Yard detective squads had been eliminated' (Reiner, *The Politics of the Police*, p. 63). G. F. Newman claims, in an extraordinary *Omnibus* (7 February 1982) (itself subject to censorship) about his 1982 Royal Court play, *Operation Bad Apple*, that Countryman had concluded with a cover-up.
116 'Why an Ex-Police Chief Could Not Watch BBC Series', *Now*, 14 March 1980.
117 David Hare in Kelly, *Alan Clarke*, p. 105.
118 *Arena*: 'When Is a Play Not a Play'.

Select Bibliography

Alvarado, Manuel and John Stewart, *Made for Television: Euston Films Limited* (London: BFI and Thames Methuen, 1985).

Bignell, Jonathan, Stephen Lacey and Madeleine Macmurragh-Kavanagh (eds), *British Television Drama: Past, Present and Future* (Basingstoke: Palgrave Macmillan, 2000).

Briggs, Asa, *The History of Broadcasting in the United Kingdom Volume V: Competition* (Oxford: Oxford University Press, 1995).

Burns, Tom, *The BBC: Public Institution and Private World* (London: Macmillan, 1977).

Cape, Ed, 'Rebalancing the Criminal Justice Process: Ethical Challenges for Criminal Defence Lawyers', *Legal Ethics* vol. 9 no. 1 (2006): 56–79.

Caughie, John, *Television Drama: Realism, Modernism, and British Culture* (Oxford: Oxford University Press, 2000).

——, *Edge of Darkness* (London: BFI, 2007).

Clarke, Alan, ' "This Is Not the Boy Scouts": Television Police Series and Definitions of Law and Order', in Tony Bennett, Colin Mercer and Janet Woollacott (eds), *Popular Culture and Social Relations* (Milton Keynes: Open University Press, 1986), pp. 219–232.

——, ' "You're Nicked": Television Police Series and the Fictional Representation of Law and Order', in Dominic Strinati and Stephen Wagg (eds), *Come on Down* (London: Routledge, 1992), pp. 232–53.

Cooke, Lez, *British Television Drama: A History* (London: BFI, 2003).

——, *Troy Kennedy Martin* (Manchester: Manchester University Press, 2007).

Cox, Barry, John Shirley and Martin Short, *The Fall of Scotland Yard* (Harmondsworth: Penguin, 1977).

Edgar, David 'What Are We Telling the Nation?', *London Review of Books*, 7 July 2005: 16–20.

Emsley, Clive, *The English Police: A Political and Social History*, 2nd edn (Harlow: Longman, 1996).

Fiddick, Peter, 'The Unfair Cop', *The Guardian*, 24 April 1978.

——, 'Police and Prison Officers Are up in Arms about How BBC Programmes like *Law and Order* Spoil Their Image: What They Want Is Censorship', *The Guardian*, 24 July 1978.

——, 'The Silent Censorship on Behalf of a Decidedly Unconfused Public', *The Guardian*, 25 June 1979, p. 10.

Freedman, Des, *Television Policies of the Labour Party 1951–2001* (London: Frank Cass, 2003).

Garnett, Tony, 'Working in the Field', in S. Rowbotham and H. Beynon (eds), *Looking at Class* (London: Rivers Oram, 2001).

Goddard, Peter, John Corner and Kay Richardson, *Public Issue Television: World in Action, 1963–98* (Manchester: Manchester University Press, 2007).

Goodwin, Andrew, Paul Kerr and Ian Macdonald (eds), *BFI Dossier 19: Drama-Documentary* (London: BFI, 1983).

Goodwin, Peter, *Television under the Tories: Broadcasting Policy 1979–1997* (London: BFI, 1998).

Hall, Stuart, Chas Critcher, Tony Jefferson, John Clarke and Brian Roberts, *Policing the Crisis* (London: Macmillan, 1978).

Hill, John, 'Interview with Ken Loach', in George McKnight (ed.), *Agent of Challenge and Defiance* (Trowbridge: Flicks Books, 1997).

Hobbs, Dick, *Doing the Business: Entrepreneurship, the Working Class, and Detectives in the East End of London* (Oxford: Oxford University Press, 1989).

——, 'Stealing Commercial Cash: From Safecracking to Armed Robbery', in F. Brookman *et al.* (eds), *Handbook on Crime* (Cullompton: Willan, 2010).

Hollingsworth, Mark and Richard Norton-Taylor, *Blacklist: The Inside Story of Political Vetting* (London: Hogarth Press, 1988).

Jacobs, Jason, *Body Trauma TV: The New Hospital Dramas* (London: BFI, 2003).

Jenkins, Steve, '*Law and Order*: "A Detective's Tale" ', *Monthly Film Bulletin* (June 1983): 161–2.

Kelly, Richard (ed.), *Alan Clarke* (London: Faber and Faber, 1998).

Kennedy Martin, Troy, '*Up the Junction* and After', *Contrast* vol. 4 no. 5/6 (1965/6): 137–41.

——, 'From "War Game" to "Law and Order" ' *Vision* vol. 4 no. 1 (April 1979): 5–7.

——, 'Sharpening the Edge of TV Drama' (McTaggart Lecture), *The Listener*, 28 August 1986: 9–12.

Kidd-Hewitt, David and Richard Osborne (eds), *Crime and Media: The Post-Modern Spectacle* (London: Pluto Press, 1995).

Lacey, Stephen, *Tony Garnett* (Manchester: Manchester University Press, 2007).

McGonville, Mike, Jacqueline Hodgson, Lee Bridges and Anita Pavlovic, *Standing Accused: The Organisation and Practices of Criminal Defence Lawyers in Britain* (Oxford: Clarendon Press, 1994).

McKibbin, Ross, 'Homage to Wilson and Callaghan', *London Review of Books* vol. 13 no. 20 (October 1991): 3–5.

McLaughlin, E., 'From Reel to Ideal: *The Blue Lamp* and the Popular Cultural Construction of the English "Bobby" ', *Crime, Media, Culture* no. 1 (2005): 11–30.

Macmurragh-Kavanagh, Madeleine, 'Boys on Top: Gender and Authorship on the BBC Wednesday Play 1964–70', *Media, Culture and Society* vol. 21 no. 3 (1999): 409–25.

——, ' "Drama into News": Strategies of Intervention in "The Wednesday Play" ', *Screen* vol. 38 no. 3 (1997): 247–59.

Mark, Sir Robert, *In the Office of Constable* (London: Collins, 1978).

Mason, Paul, 'Prime Time Punishment: The British Prison and Television', in David Kidd-Hewitt and Richard Osborne (eds), *Crime and Media: The Post-Modern Spectacle* (London: Pluto Press, 1995).

Milne, Alastair, *DG Memoirs of a British Broadcaster* (London: Hodder and Stoughton, 1988).

Mulvey, Laura and Jamie Sexton (eds), *Experimental Television* (Manchester: Manchester University Press, 2007).

Newman, G. F., *Law & Order* (London: Granada Publishing, 1984).

——, *Sir, You Bastard* (London: New English Library, 1971 [1970]).

——, *The Guvnor* (London: Hart-Davis MacGibbon, 1977).

O'Sullivan, Sean, 'UK Policing and Its Television Portrayal: 'Law and Order' Ideology or Modernizing Agenda?', *Howard Journal of Criminal Justice* vol. 44 no. 5 (2005): 504–26.

Paget, Derek, *No Other Way to Tell It: Dramadoc/Docudrama on Television* (Manchester: Manchester University Press, 1998).

Porter, Vincent, 'The Context of Creativity: Ealing Studios and Hammer Films', in James Curran and Vincent Porter (eds), *British Cinema History* (London: Weidenfeld and Nicolson, 1983).

Rawlings, Philip, *Crime and Power: A History of Criminal Justice 1688–1998* (Harlow: Longman, 1999).

——, *Policing: A Short History* (Cullompton: Willan, 2002).

Reiner, Robert, *The Politics of the Police*, 3rd edn (Oxford: Oxford University Press, 2000).

——, *Law and Order: An Honest Citizen's Guide to Crime and Control* (Cambridge: Polity Press, 2008).

Rolinson, Dave, *Alan Clarke* (Manchester: Manchester University Press, 2005).

Screen Education, Special Issue on *The Sweeney*, 1976.

Sexton, Jamie, '"Televerité" Hits Britain: Documentary, Drama and the Growth of 16mm Filmmaking in British Television', *Screen* vol. 44 no. 4 (2003): 429–44.

Sparks, Richard, *Television and the Drama of Crime* (Buckingham: Open University Press, 1992).

Sutton, Shaun, *The Largest Theatre in the World: Thirty Years of Television Drama* (London: BBC, 1982).

Sydney-Smith, Susan, *Beyond Dixon of Dock Green: Early British Police Series* (London: I. B. Tauris, 2002).

Taylor, Laurie, 'Partners in Crime', *New Society*, 27 April 1978.

Thomas, James, '"Bound by History:" The Winter of Discontent in British Politics, 1979–2004', *Media Culture and Society* vol. 29 no. 2 (2007): 263–83.

Thompson, E. P., *Writing by Candlelight* (London: Merlin Press, 1980).

Credits

Law and Order

United Kingdom/1978

written by
G. F. Newman
directed by
Leslie Blair
produced by
Tony Garnett

photography
John Else
film recordist, eps 1, 2, 3
John Murphy
film recording, ep. 4
Malcolm Webberly
camera assistant, ep. 4
Paul Godley
film editor
Don Fairservice
designer
Austen Spriggs

production assistants
Raymond Day
Christopher Cameron
production unit manager
Elizabeth Small
make-up artist
Jean Steward, eps 1, 2, 3
Frances Needham, ep. 4
costume designer
Prue Handley
dubbing mixer
John C. C. Hale, eps 1, 2, 3
dubbing editor
Ann Lalic, ep. 4
film recordists
Doug Mawson
John Pritchard

cast

Law and Order: 'A Detective's Tale'
Derek Martin
DI Fred Pyall
Ken Campbell
Alex Gladwell
Alan Ford
Clifford Harding
Roy Sone
Micky Fielder
Billy Cornelius
DS Eric Lethridge
Fred Haggerty
DCI Tony Simmons
Dominic Allan
DCI Chatt (A10)
Mike Horsburgh
DI Graham McHale
Terry Walsh
DI John Redvers
Shaun Curry
DI Alan Welch
David Sterne
DI Maurice Head
Jan Harding
Det-Supt Ernie Jeymer
Tom De-Ville
DI Frank Polden
Douglas Sheldon
DS Jack Barcy
Robert Oates
DC Warren Salter
Colin Howells
DC Roger Humphries
Geoffrey Todd
DC Peter Fenton
Alan (Nobby) Clarke
DC Ray Jenkins
John Hogan
DS Ian Middlewick
David Stockton
DS Tony Shields
Chris Hallam
DS Lewis
Stewart Harwood
PC Malcolm
Byron Sotoris
Duty Sergeant
Mark Holmes
Duty Sergeant
Charles Cork
Terry Clark
Stanley Price
Brian Finch
Billy Dean
David Shepley
Steve Kelly
Maurice Dickenson
Cy Wallace
Billy Little
Michael Sheard
Insurance assessor
Val Clover
telephonist
David Harris
witness

Law and Order: 'A Villain's Tale'
Peter Dean
Jack Lynn
Derek Martin
DI Fred Pyall
Deirdre Costello
Cathy Lynn
Alan Ford
Clifford Harding
Roy Sone
Micky Fielder
Billy Cornelius
DS Eric Lethridge
Steve Ismay
Bobby Shaw
Barry Summerford
John Tully
Alan Davidson
Benny Isaacs
Tony Barouch
Colin Coleman
Alf Coster
Philip Hayes
John Bardon
Del Rogers
Mike Cummings
Tommy Haines

Fred Haggerty
DCI Tony Simmons
Mike Horsburgh
DI Graham McHale
Douglas Sheldon
DS Jack Barcy
Robert Oates
DC Warren Salter
Colin Howells
DC Roger Humphries
Geoffrey Todd
DC Peter Fenton
Alan (Nobby) Clarke
DC Ray Jenkins
Johnny Feltwell
DC Matthew Hall
Eric Kent
DI Frank Kenley
Jason White
DC Simon Brent
Peter Craze
TDC Peter Footring
Martin Gordon
Mr English
Frank Henson
John Blackburn
Security guards
John Chissick
Andy
Barney Carroll
Alan
Bob Sutherland
Trevor Foley
Pat Curtis
Mrs Coleman
Franklyn Whiteley
Bank manager
Debby Martin
Bank clerk
Buddy Prince
Club doorman
Reg Thomason
Milkman
Jack Eden
Snooker hall barman
John Cannon
Duty Sergeant
Jason James
Identity parade inspector
Philip Lennard
Magistrate
Bruce Wyllie
Lynn's solicitor
Peter Hannon
Warrant officer

Law and Order: 'A Brief's Tale'
Ken Campbell
Alex Gladwell
Peter Dean
Jack Lynn
Deirdre Costello
Cathy Lynn
Derek Martin
DI Fred Pyall
Billy Cornelius
DS Eric Lethridge
André Van Gyseghem
Judge Robert Quigley
Michael Griffiths
Horace McMillan, QC
Peter Welch
Brian Harpenden-Smith, QC
Terence Bayler
Michael Messick, QC
Jeffrey Segal
Stanley Eaton, QC
Barry Summerford
John Tully
Alan Davidson
Benny Isaacs
Tony Barouch
Colin Coleman
Alan Ford
Clifford Harding
John Feltwell
DC Matthew Hall
Jason White
DC Simon Brent
Frank Henson
Frank Ryan
Martin Gordon
Mr English
Jean Leppard
Margaret Lloyd
Peter Craze
TDC Peter Footring
Mike Cummings
Tommy Haines
Anthony Allen
McMillan's junior
Stanley McGeagh
Gladwell's clerk
Eric Rainer
Ray Gatenby
Clerks of the court
George Romanov
Court usher
Marion Park
Jury forewoman
Laurence Harrington
Derek Wisby
Terry Plummer
DI Dave Mason
Beryl Martin
Gladwell's secretary
Fred Haggerty
DCI Tony Simmons
Eric Kent
DI Frank Kenley
Eric French
PC in café
Eric Mason
DS Ted Collinson
Brian Hawksley
Magistrate
Michael Haughey
Arthur Rawlings
Gino Melvazzi
Waiter
James Charlton
Warder in Old Bailey

Law and Order: 'A Prisoner's Tale'
Peter Dean
Jack Lynn
Deirdre Costello
Cathy Lynn
Edward Cast
Governor Maudling
Roger Booth
Chief Officer Carne
Farrell Sheridan
Principal Officer McClean
Gil Sutherland
Principal Officer Allen
Harry Walker
Dr Eynshaw
P. H. Moriarty
Stephen Collins
Robert Bill
Micky Dunkerton
Bruce White
Bob Mark
Reginald Stewart
Alan Thompson
Martyn Jacobs
Brian Smith
Myles Reithermann
Mervyn Latimer
Gilbert McIntyre
Baylis
Ronald Clarke
Brian Lang

Terence Orr
Simon Menzies
Lloyd McGuire
PO Jordan
Dave Atkins
PO Dorman
Reg Turner
PO Allison
Bill Rourke
PO Cassidy
Ronan Paterson
PO Westbury
Graham Gough
PO Powell
Alan Stanford
PO Maitland
Tony Wilson
PO Evans
Laurence Foster
Sr Officer Walters
Max Latimer
Colin Taylor
Prison officers, visiting room
Steve Emerson
Mark Warren
Prison officers, legal visiting room
Ian P. Munro
Alf Roberts
Prison officers, punishment block
Ken Campbell
Alex Gladwell
Stanley McGeagh
Trevor Reid
Dominic Allan
Inspector Chatt (A10)
Terry Yorke
Police Sergeant
Stanley Illsley
Pauline Wynn
Visiting committee
Harry Landis
MP

transmission history
'A Detective's Tale'
BBC2 tx 6 April 1978 (9 pm)

'A Villain's Tale'
BBC2 tx 13 April 1978 (9 pm)

'A Brief's Tale'
BBC2 tx 20 April 1978 (9 pm)

'A Prisoner's Tale'
BBC2 tx 27 April 1978 (9 pm)

Repeated
'Playhouse Presents'
BBC2 tx 9 March 1980 (10.25 pm), 16 March 1980 (10.25 pm), 23 March 1980 (10.05 pm), 30 March 1980 (10.30 pm)

Screened at the National Film Theatre in London, presented by the National Film Archive, on Saturday 27 October 1979, followed by discussion with Tony Garnett, G. F. Newman and other members of the production team.

'A Detective's Tale' released as 16mm print by the British Film Institute, May 1983.

DVD released, March 2008: *G. F. Newman's Law and Order*, BBC Worldwide Ltd, distributed under licence by 2Entertain, 2008.

Repeated on BBC4 (Satellite channel, Freeview), 24 March 2009 (10.50 pm), 31 March 2009 (10.50 pm), 7 April 2009 (10.50 pm), 14 April 2009 (10.45 pm).

There are some anomalies in the spelling of the detective's name. It is spelt Pyall in the BBC films, in both the end credits and the *Radio Times*, but Pyle in the subsequent novel version.

Index

Notes:
Films/programmes indexed by title are UK TV unless otherwise indicated.
Page numbers in **bold** indicate detailed analysis; those in *italics* denote illustrations; *n* = endnote.

Also Published:

Buffy the Vampire Slayer
Anne Billson

Civilisation
Jonathan Conlin

Cracker
Mark Duguid

CSI: Crime Scene Investigation
Steven Cohan

Doctor Who
Kim Newman

Edge of Darkness
John Caughie

The League of Gentlemen
Leon Hunt

The Likely Lads
Phil Wickham

The Office
Ben Walters

Our Friends in the North
Michael Eaton

Prime Suspect
Deborah Jermyn

Queer as Folk
Glyn Davis

Seinfeld
Nicholas Mirzoeff

Seven Up
Stella Bruzzi

The Singing Detective
Glen Creeber

Star Trek
Ina Rae Hark

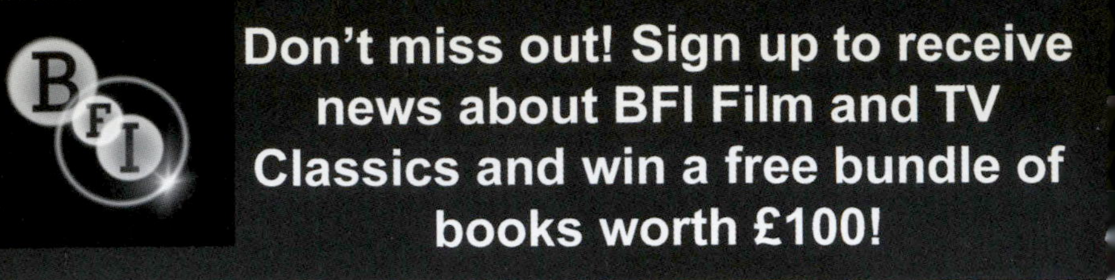
Don't miss out! Sign up to receive news about BFI Film and TV Classics and win a free bundle of books worth £100!

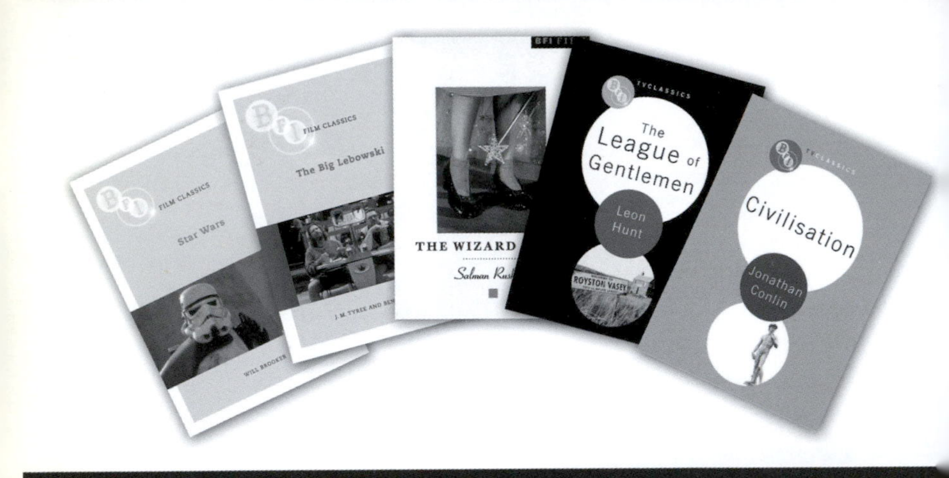
FILM CLASSICS
Star Wars
WILL BROOKER
FILM CLASSICS
The Big Lebowski
THE WIZARD
TV CLASSICS
The League of Gentlemen
Leon Hunt
ROYSTON VASEY
Civilisation
Jonathan Conlin

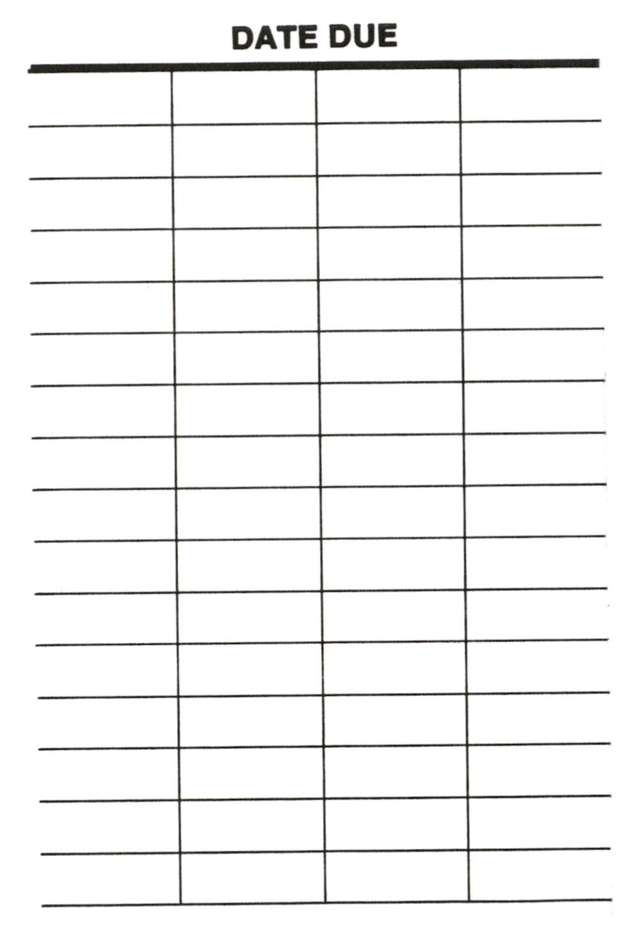